SPIRALIZE AND THRIVE

Skyhorse Publishing books may be purchased in bulk at special discounts for sales promotion, corporate gifts, fund-raising, or educational purposes. Special editions can also be created to specifications. For details, contact the Special Sales Department, Skyhorse Publishing, 307 West 36th Street, 11th Floor, New York, NY 10018 or info@skyhorsepublishing.com.

Skyhorse® and Skyhorse Publishing® are registered trademarks of Skyhorse Publishing, Inc.®, a Delaware corporation.

Visit our website at www.skyhorsepublishing.com.

10 9 8 7 6 5 4 3 2 1

Library of Congress Cataloging-in-Publication Data is available on file.

Cover design by Jane Sheppard
Cover photo by Dalila Tarhuni

Print ISBN: 978-1-5107-0899-0
Ebook ISBN: 978-1-5107-0901-0

Printed in China

SPIRALIZE AND THRIVE

100 Vibrant Vegetable-Based Recipes for Starters, Salads, Soups, Suppers, and More

DALILA TARHUNI

Skyhorse Publishing

CONTENTS

INTRODUCTION: WHY SPIRALIZE?

Including plenty of fresh, ideally locally-grown and organic produce in your daily diet is essential for good health and one simple and fun way of achieving that is by spiralizing. A Japanese invention, the spiralizer is a safer version of a mandoline slicer that produces noodle or ribbon-like strands from a variety of vegetables and fruits. Over the last few years, the spiralizer's popularity has soared and it has quickly become a must-have kitchen tool, particularly for the health conscious.

Whether you are looking to incorporate more vegetables and fruit in your family's diet or following gluten free, Paleo, or another special diet lifestyle, this wonderful gadget is indispensable and worth investing in.

Cutting back on calories and refined carbs in order to achieve or maintain a healthy weight is significantly easier if you substitute rice or grain-based pasta and couscous with spiralized vegetables. The following table shows how the nutritional value of 100 grams (3.5 ounces) cooked spiralized zucchini compares to 100 g (3.5 ounces) cooked couscous, quinoa, white and brown rice, and both wheat and whole wheat spaghetti.

3.5 ounces (100g), cooked	Calories	Carbs (g)	Protein (g)	Fat (g)	Sodium (mg)
Zucchini	16	4	1	0	3
Couscous	112	23	4	0	5
Quinoa	120	21	4	2	7
Rice, brown	112	24	2	1	1
Rice, white	130	29	2	0	0
Spaghetti, wheat	158	31	6	0	1
Spaghetti, whole wheat	124	27	5	1	3

Nutritional Information of Spiralized Vegetables and Fruits*

Ingredient (100 g)	Calories	Carbs (g)	Protein(g)	Fat (g)	Sodium (mg)
Apples	48	13	0	0	0
Beets	44	10	2	0	77
Broccoli Stems	34	7	2	0	40
Butternut squash	40	12	1	0	4
Carrots	35	8	1	0	58
Celery root	27	6	1	0	61
Chayote squash	24	5	1	0	1
Cucumbers	15	4	1	0	2
Daikon radish	17	3	1	0	13
Dragon fruit	60	9	2	1.5	60
Eddoe	120	26.2	1.4	0.2	trace
Jicama	38	9	1	0	4
Kohlrabi	29	7	2	0	21
Korean radish	17	3	1	0	13
Onions	44	10	1	0	3
Parsnips	71	17	1	0	10
Pears	58	15	0	0	1
Persimmons	70	19	1	0	1
Plantains	116	31	1	0	5
Potatoes	86	20	2	0	5
Quinces	57	15	0	0	4
Red and Green Cabbage	23	6	1	0	8
Rutabaga	39	9	1	0	20
Shallots	72	17	3	0	12
Sweet potatoes	76	18	1	0	27
Taro	142	35	1	0	15
Turnips	22	5	1	0	16
Yucca	160	38	1	0	14
Zucchini	16	4	1	0	3

*The above nutritional data was calculated using the USDA National Nutrient Database for Standard Reference and is for informational purpose only.

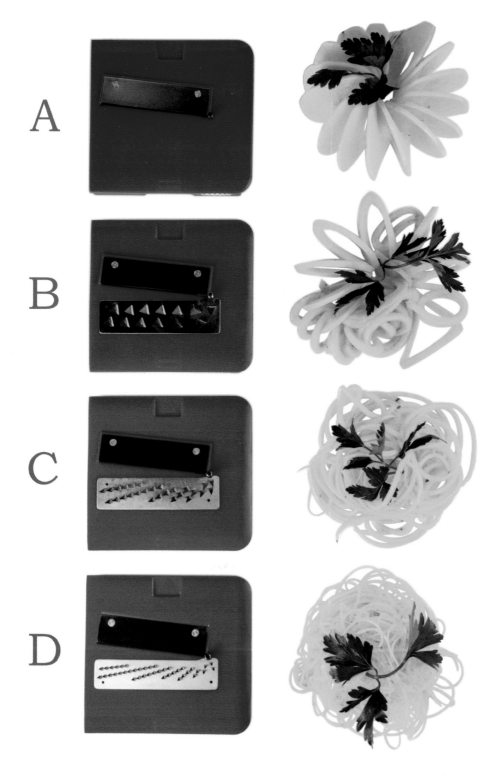

BLADE TYPES AND USES

Although there is a huge variety of spiralizers on the market, most of them come with three to five stainless-steel blades, either adjustable or interchangeable, that include a straight/flat blade and shredding blades in different sizes. Some of the smaller, hand-held spiralizers/vegetable cutters come with two sizes of julienne blades only.

Below are the four blades used for creating the recipes in this book, but if your spiralizer comes with different ones, simply adjust the cut and thickness of the vegetables and fruit to the blades you have.

A – Straight/Flat Blade

This is the most versatile blade. It creates long ribbon strands, similar to pappardelle pasta, and it can also shred or slice into crescents, rounds, or even an accordion shapes. For crescents, make lengthwise cuts on two opposite sides of the vegetable or fruit, without going through the center, and for rounds, make just one cut. For an accordion cut, before proceeding, pierce the vegetable or fruit with the metal pin provided by some manufacturers or with a small skewer. This works with some spiralizers only.

B – Chipper Blade

Use this blade for thick, round, spiral strands similar to fettuccine. It is ideal for curly fries.

C – Shredder/Julienne Blade

The most popular blade, it produces thin, round spaghetti-like spirals and works with most firm vegetables and fruit.

D – Fine Shredder/Julienne Blade

Use this blade to make long strands of angel hair noodles. It works well with vegetables smaller in diameter.

Care

Wash the blades, preferably immediately after use, under warm water with a mild detergent, scrubbing with a hard brush, or use a soap dispensing dish brush. Some manufacturers recommend placing the blades on the upper rack of a dishwasher.

IMPORTANT: Read the manufacturer's instructions carefully and thoroughly before first use. The blades are extremely sharp, so always handle with caution and never touch directly.

COOKED VS. RAW VEGETABLES AND FRUITS

Without a doubt, it is best to keep a balanced intake of both cooked and raw fresh, high-quality produce. However, depending on the vegetables, some are more nutritious when cooked while others may lose valuable vitamins when heated and are therefore healthier eaten raw.

If you are watching your weight, eating raw fruits and vegetables will fill you up better as they are bulkier. The water-soluble (B and C) vitamins are heat-sensitive and may decrease with cooking while the fat-soluble vitamins (A, D, E, and K) are not affected.

For example, cooking the carrots makes the beta-carotene easier to absorb. Cruciferous vegetables, like cabbage and broccoli, are easier to digest when cooked, although broccoli could also be served raw as the heat destroys one of its important enzymes, myrosinase. The anti-inflammatory properties of onions increase when cooked, while garlic is best eaten raw. Avoid raw potatoes as they contain a toxin called solanine, and the starch in raw potatoes causes digestive problems. Eddoes are poisonous in large quantities if consumed raw.

Cooking times depend on the thickness of the noodles and method of cooking. Sautéing the spiralized vegetables or fruit in a heavy-bottomed skillet with a little oil, broth, or water for a few minutes works best, but steaming, simmering, microwaving, and baking, are also great options. Cook noodles until they are just tender but still retain some crunch, then remove immediately from the heat. To microwave, combine spiralized vegetables in a bowl and add a little water; drain the water and dry on paper towels before serving. Angel hair noodles don't need any cooking, and are usually best in salads or for garnishes; if using in hot soups, add at the end and turn off the heat. Zucchini noodles need very little cooking, about 2 minutes, so you may just pour the hot sauce over them before serving. Taro root and eddoes should be simmered in water until fully cooked.

Following is a quick reference of the approximate cooking times for sautéing, steaming, or simmering spiralized vegetables and fruits. Baking times normally range between 10 to 15 minutes, depending on the cut, and microwaving takes 1–3 minutes, again depending on the thickness and the vegetables.

Also included below are the best substitutes with other spiralizable ingredients.

Ingredient	Cooked or Raw	Cooking times (minutes)	Blades	Preparations, Varieties, and Substitutes
Apples	Both	4–5	A, B, C	Remove stem (may core for slicing) and slice off ends. All varieties are interchangeable in raw recipes; for baking use firm apples, such as Pink Lady, Honeycrisp, Jonathans, Melrose, or Granny Smith.
Beets	Both	5–7	All	Peel and slice off ends. All varieties (red, golden, or chioggia) are interchangeable.
Black radish	Both	5–7	All	Scrub well or peel and slice off ends; interchangeable with turnip and rutabaga.
Broccoli Stems	Both	5–7	C, D	Trim and slice off ends; interchangeable with kohlrabi.
Butternut squash	Cooked	6–8	All	Only the neck spiralizes. Peel and slice off ends; interchangeable with sweet potatoes.
Cabbage	Both	5–7	A	Choose small, tight red or green cabbage heads, halved or quartered.
Carrots	Both	5–7	All	Choose large carrots, any variety; peel and slice off ends.
Celery root	Both	5–7	All	Peel and slice off ends; raw celery root is interchangeable with Daikon radish and cooked with rutabaga and turnips.
Chayote squash	Both	2–3	All	Slice ends off and remove excess moisture with kitchen paper towels after spiralizing. Interchangeable with any summer squash.
Cucumbers	Raw	NA	All	Slice off ends and remove excess moisture with kitchen paper towels after spiralizing. Interchangeable with chayote, zucchini, and jicama.

(*continued on nxt page*)

Ingredient	Cooked or Raw	Cooking times (minutes)	Blades	Preparations, Varieties, and Substitutes
Daikon radish	Both	5–7	All	Peel, slice ends off, and cut in 5–6-inch pieces if too long. Interchangeable with Korean radish and jicama.
Dragon fruit	Raw	NA	B, C	Slice off ends and peel; substitute with pears if not available.
Eddoe	Cooked	7–9	A, B, C	Wear gloves when handling to prevent skin irritation and peel. Interchangeable with taro root, potatoes, and malanga; simmer in water.
Jerusalem artichoke (sunchoke, sunroot, or topinambur)	Cooked		A, B, C	Either scrub well or peel and slice off ends; interchangeable with jicama and potatoes.
Jicama	Both	5–7	All	Peel, slice ends off, and cut in half lengthwise if too large. Interchangeable with Jerusalem artichokes and Daikon radish.
Kohlrabi	Both	6–7	All	Peel and slice off ends and cut in half lengthwise if too large; interchangeable with turnip, celery root, broccoli stems, and parsnips.
Korean radish	Both	5–7	All	Peel and slice ends off; cut in half if too long. Interchangeable with Daikon radish.
Malanga	Cooked	6–8	A, B, C	Interchangeable with potatoes, taro, eddoes, and sweet potatoes.
Onions	Both	4–5	A, B, C	Peel and slice off ends; all varieties are interchangeable.
Parsnips	Cooked	6–8	A, B, C	Peel and slice off ends; interchangeable with turnip or celery root.
Pears	Both	4–5	A, B. C	Remove stem, may core for slicing; substitute with apples.

Ingredient	Cooked or Raw	Cooking times (minutes)	Blades	Preparations, Varieties, and Substitutes
Persimmons	Both	5–6	A, B, C	Peel and slice off ends; substitute raw with apples and cooked with butternut squash.
Plantains	Cooked	6–8	A, B, C	Slice off ends and peel.
Potatoes	Cooked	7–8	All	Peel and slice off ends; interchangeable with sweet potatoes, yucca, taro, eddoes, and malanga.
Quinces	Both	6–7	A	Slice off ends and peel; substitute with Bartlett pears or apples.
Rutabaga (swede, yellow turnip)	Cooked	6–7	All	Peel and slice off ends; interchangeable with turnip, celeriac, kohlrabi, and black radish.
Shallots	Both	3–4	A	Peel and slice ends off; use large shallots; substitute with red onions.
Sweet potatoes	Cooked	6–7	All	Peel and slice off ends. All sweet potato varieties are interchangeable.
Taro root (dasheen)	Cooked	6–8	A, B, C	Peel and slice ends off and simmer in water. Interchangeable with potatoes, malanga, and eddoes.
Turnips	Both	6–7	All	Peel and slice off ends, interchangeable with rutabaga, kohlrabi, celery root, black radish, and Daikon radish.
Yucca (cassava)	Cooked		A, B, C	Peel and slice off ends; cut in smaller pieces if too long. Interchangeable with potatoes.
Zucchini	Both	2–3	All	Interchangeable with all other squash varieties. Slice off ends and cut in half if too long.

MAKING VEGETABLE RICE OR COUSCOUS

To make rice or couscous, first spiralize the ingredients, then pulse in a food processor or a blender to the desired size. Use Blade C for smaller rice grains or North African couscous, and Blade B for larger grains, such as risotto rice or Israeli couscous.

To cook, for each cup of vegetable rice, heat ½ to 1 tablespoon olive oil over a medium heat and cook, stirring frequently, for 5–6 minutes, or until the rice is just tender, but retains some bite. If it starts sticking to the bottom of the skillet, add a little water or broth. This will also make the rice fluffier. Some of the riced vegetables, such as beets, carrots, zucchini, jicama, and radishes, may be served raw.

The following vegetables are most suitable for ricing:

- Beets
- Butternut squash
- Carrots
- Celery root
- Daikon radish
- Jicama
- Kohlrabi
- Korean radish

- Parsnips
- Plantains
- Potatoes
- Rutabaga
- Sweet potatoes
- Turnips
- Zucchini

TIPS FOR BEST RESULTS

- Choose firm, straight vegetables, preferably at least 2 inches in diameter. Thinner vegetables will yield shorter and often broken noodles.

- Whenever possible, spiralize fruit or vegetables just before you need them. You could save time by spiralizing in bulk and storing in airtight containers in the fridge for 2–3 days. To keep the vegetables crisp, store them in water. Adding a squeeze of fresh lemon juice to the water will prevent browning, especially in apples, pears, quinces, parsnips, celery root, and Daikon radishes.

- Pat dry moist vegetables such as zucchini, radishes, chayote, and cucumbers with paper towels before cooking and use thick sauces with vegetable pasta.

- Do not overcook the spiralized vegetables.

SAUCES

AVOCADO SAUCE

Servings 8
Prep time: 5 minutes
Cooking time: None

Ingredients:

3 tablespoons sour cream or plain Greek
    yogurt
1 garlic clove, crushed
1 medium ripe avocado, pitted and diced
2–3 tablespoons lime juice, to taste
A dash of hot sauce (more to taste)
Sea salt and freshly ground black pepper,
    to taste

Directions:

In a blender or food processor, combine all of the sauce ingredients and blend until very smooth, adding a splash of water if too thick.

Serve with the *Breakfast Burrito Cups*, (page 22**),** or drizzle over raw or cooked zucchini noodles for a quick meal. It is also great as a salad dressing and will keep in the fridge in a lidded container for up to 3 days.

✔ Gluten-free ✔ Wheat-free
✔ Low fat ✔ Low carb

Nutrition facts per serving for the sauce (20 g):

calories 27 | total carbs 2g | protein 0g | total fat 2g | cholesterol 0mg | sodium 7mg

ORANGE GINGER SAUCE

Servings 8
Prep time: 5 minutes
Cooking time: None

Ingredients:

2 tablespoons olive oil
1 garlic clove, crushed
½ teaspoon ginger, grated
¾ cup orange juice
1 tablespoon sugar free orange marmalade
3 tablespoons fresh parsley, chopped
Sea salt and freshly ground black pepper

✔ Gluten-free ✔ Dairy-free
✔ Paleo ✔ Wheat-free
✔ Low fat

Nutrition facts per serving for the sauce (40 g):

calories 63 | total carbs 6g | protein 0g | total fat 5g | cholesterol 0mg | sodium 3mg

Directions:

Heat olive oil in saucepan over medium heat. Add garlic and ginger and stir for 30 seconds, until fragrant. Pour in orange juice, add marmalade, season, and bring to a boil; reduce heat and let simmer until the liquid is reduced by half and thickened. Stir in parsley.

Serve with *Sweet Potato-Wrapped Tilapia with Orange Sauce* (page 90), or with other grilled or baked white fish or chicken.

CAPER SAUCE

Servings 8
Prep time: 5 minutes
Cooking time: 8–10 minutes

Ingredients:

2 tablespoons unsalted butter
2 shallots, peeled and finely chopped
2–3 salt-cured anchovy fillets, washed and
   chopped (optional)
¼ cup capers, drained and roughly chopped
¼ cup fresh parsley, finely chopped
1 cup low-sodium chicken or lamb stock
   (more as needed)

Sea salt and freshly ground black pepper, to
   taste
1½ tablespoons arrowroot powder, mixed
   with ¼ cup water
Fresh lemon juice, to taste
A drizzle of honey, to taste

Directions:

Melt butter in a medium saucepan over medium heat; add shallots and anchovies and
sauté until softened, about 2–3 minutes. Stir in capers and parsley and pour in the
stock. Season with salt and pepper and bring to a boil. Reduce heat and cook for about
4–5 minutes, then stir in the arrowroot slurry. Cook for 1–2 minutes, adding more stock
if necessary, to get a medium thick sauce consistency. Adjust the taste with lemon juice
and a drizzle of honey.

It complements the *Citrus and Garlic Roasted Lamb with Parsnip Rice* (page 136) nicely,
and also works well with roasted or grilled chicken.

✔ Gluten-free ✔ Wheat-free
✔ Low fat ✔ Low carb

Nutrition facts per serving for the
sauce (50 g):

calories 37 | total carbs 3g
| protein 1g | total fat 3g |
cholesterol 8mg | sodium 137mg

ROASTED GARLIC AND MINT PESTO

Servings 8–10
Prep time: 5 minutes
Cooking time: 25–30 minutes

Ingredients:

1 garlic bulb
⅓ cup extra virgin olive oil
3 tablespoons shelled pistachios
3 tablespoons cashews
⅔ packed cup fresh mint leaves
⅓ cup fresh parsley
Juice and zest of 1 lemon
Sea salt and freshly ground black pepper

✔ Gluten-free   ✔ Dairy-free
✔ Paleo   ✔ Wheat-free
✔ Low fat   ✔ High protein
✔ Low carb

Nutrition facts per serving for the pesto sauce (10 g):

calories 46 | total carbs 1g
| protein 1g | total fat 5g |
cholesterol 0mg |
sodium 1mg

Directions:

Preheat oven to 425°F. Slice off the top of the garlic bulb, brush generously with olive oil, and wrap in a piece of aluminium foil. Place on a baking sheet and bake for about 25–30 minutes, until tender; let cool for a few minutes before gently squeezing the cloves out. Add roasted garlic to a blender or food processor together with the rest of the pesto ingredients. Pulse until well combined, season with salt and pepper to taste, and adjust the consistency to your liking by adding a little water. Transfer to a bowl and set aside.

Serve the pesto sauce with the *Lamb Souvlaki and Rutabaga Rice* (page 138), use in sandwiches and dips, or stir it into cooked spiralized vegetable pasta. Keeps refrigerated for up to 5 days.

ROASTED PEPPER SAUCE

Servings 8
Prep time: 10 minutes
Cooking time: 45–50 minutes

Ingredients:

3 orange or red large bell peppers*
1 tablespoon extra virgin olive oil
1–2 garlic cloves, crushed
1 fresh thyme sprig
Dash of cayenne pepper
Vegetable stock, as needed

A drizzle of honey
Sea salt and freshly grated black pepper,
* to taste*

*Or substitute with jarred roasted peppers

Directions:

Place peppers on a rimmed baking sheet and roast for about 35–40 minutes, or until the skins are blackened. Carefully transfer peppers to a glass bowl or container, cover the bowl with plastic wrap and let cool for 5–10 minutes. Skip this step if using jarred roasted peppers.

Peel and seed the peppers and chop roughly; strain any juices left in the bowl and set aside.

Heat the olive oil in a medium skillet over a medium-high heat. Add garlic, peppers, and thyme sprig and cook, stirring often, for 2–3 minutes. Add ½ cup of the pepper juices or vegetable stock; season to taste with salt, pepper, and a dash of cayenne. Bring to a boil; cover with a lid and reduce heat to low. Simmer, covered, for 8–10 minutes until slightly thickened. Remove thyme sprig and transfer mixture to a blender; pulse until smooth, adding a little vegetable stock if needed, to get a thick sauce consistency. Adjust seasoning and stir in a little honey if the sauce tastes a little bitter. Transfer sauce to a bowl, cover with a plastic wrap, and set aside.

Serve the sauce with the *Citrus Chicken with Ratatouille Timbales* (page 110), or use to garnish other chicken, meat, or vegetable dishes.

✔ Gluten-free ✔ Dairy-free
✔ Paleo ✔ Wheat-free
✔ Low fat ✔ Low carb

Nutrition facts per serving for the sauce (40 g):

calories 20 | total carbs 2g | protein 0g | total fat 1g | cholesterol 0mg | sodium 7mg

SPICY MANGO AND GREEN TEA DIPPING SAUCE

Servings 4-6
Prep Time: 7 minutes
Cooking Time: None

Ingredients:

2 green tea bags
1 ripe mango, pitted, peeled, and diced
Juice and zest from 1 lime
1 small fresh red chili, seeded and finely chopped
1 garlic clove, minced
1 tablespoon sweet chili sauce
2–3 tablespoons rice vinegar, to taste
1 teaspoon ginger, finely grated
1–2 teaspoons honey, to taste
1 teaspoon fish sauce
1 tablespoon sesame seeds oil
2 teaspoons low-sodium soy sauce or coconut aminos
3–4 tablespoons cilantro, finely chopped

Directions:

Steep green tea bags in ½ cup hot water for about 5 minutes; discard the bags and let cool down for 5 minutes.

In a blender, combine green tea with the remaining sauce ingredients except cilantro; blend until smooth, adjust seasoning, and transfer to a bowl. Stir in chopped cilantro, adjust seasoning, and refrigerate until needed.

Serve with the *Vietnamese Summer Rolls* (page 174), or with other Asian dishes.

✔ Gluten-free   ✔ Dairy-free
✔ Wheat-free   ✔ Low fat
✔ Low carb

Nutrition facts per serving for the sauce (30 g):

calories 17 | total carbs 4g | protein 0g | total fat 0g | cholesterol 0mg | sodium 30mg

APPLE TZATZIKI

Serves 4-6
Prep Time: 7 minutes
Cooking Time: None

Ingredients:

1 Granny Smith apple, peeled, cored,
    spiralized with Blade C and cut into
    1-inch strings
2 tablespoons lemon juice
2 small cucumbers, trimmed, spiralized with
    Blade C, and cut into 1-inch strings
1 cup plain Greek yogurt
A drizzle of honey
A pinch of cayenne
1 tablespoon fresh mint, finely chopped
1 tablespoon extra virgin olive oil
Sea salt and freshly ground black pepper, to
    taste

Directions:

Place spiralized apple, lemon juice, and cucumber in a fine-meshed strainer over a bowl and sprinkle with a little salt; let stand for 10–15 minutes. Gently squeeze out any moisture and transfer to a bowl. Add yogurt, honey, cayenne, and mint and stir with a fork to combine; season to taste and drizzle a little olive oil on top. Refrigerate until needed.

Serve with the *Chickpea and Vegetable Fritters* (page 180), or with other Mediterranean or Middle-Eastern dishes.

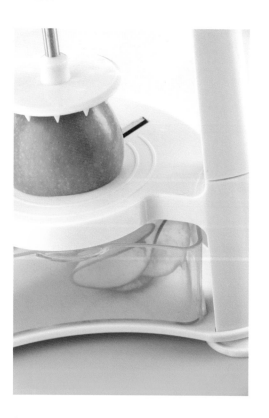

✔ Gluten-free   ✔ Wheat-free
✔ Low fat   ✔ Low carb

Nutrition facts per serving for tzatziki (45 g):

calories 30 | total carbs 3g | protein 1g | total fat 1g | cholesterol 1mg | sodium 15mg

TAHINI-YOGURT SAUCE

Servings 6
Prep Time: 20 minutes
Cooking Time: None

Ingredients:

½ cup Greek yogurt
1½ tablespoons tahini
1 garlic clove, minced
1 teaspoon raw honey
⅛ teaspoon of each cayenne pepper and
    ground cumin
1 tablespoon olive oil
2–3 tablespoons lime juice
Sea salt and freshly ground black pepper, to taste

✔ Gluten-free ✔ Wheat-free
✔ Low fat   ✔ Low carb

Directions:

Place all sauce ingredients in a blender and pulse until smooth; adjust seasoning and set aside.

Serve with *Imam Bayildi with Zucchini Pasta* (page 154), or with other Mediterranean or Middle-Eastern dishes.

Nutrition facts per serving for the sauce (15 g):

calories 24 | total carbs 1g | protein 1g | total fat 2g | cholesterol 1mg | sodium 6mg

ROSEMARY MARINADE

Servings 8
Prep time: 5 minutes
Cooking time: 25–30 minutes

Ingredients:

Juice and zest from 1 large lemon
3 tablespoons extra virgin olive oil
2 fresh bay leaves
5 garlic cloves, peeled and roughly chopped
1½ tablespoons fresh rosemary leaves,
    chopped
Sea salt and freshly ground black pepper
⅓ cup white wine (optional)
1 small chili pepper, chopped (optional)

Directions:

In a food processor or blender, combine all marinade ingredients and blitz until smooth; pour over your dish and stir to coat well. Cover and refrigerate for 1–2 hours; remove your dish of choice and discard the marinade.

Use this to marinate lamb, pork, or chicken; for example, the *Rosemary-Lemon Chicken with Carrot and Sweet Potato Rotini* (page 122).

✔ Gluten-free ✔ Dairy-free ✔ Paleo ✔ Wheat-free ✔ Low fat ✔ Low carb

CREAMY PEAS AND AVOCADO DIP

Serves 8-10
Prep Time: 20 minutes
Cooking Time: None

Ingredients:

1 ripe avocado
1 cup frozen peas
1 handful watercress
1 handful dandelion leaves
1 handful arugula
3 tablespoons lemon juice
¼ cup olive oil
3 tablespoons raw pine nuts
2 garlic cloves, crushed
Sea salt and freshly ground black pepper,
    to taste

Directions:

Place all dip ingredients in a blender or food processor and blend to a smooth puree. Add a little water to adjust thickness.

Serve with *Kohlrabi, Celery Root and Quinoa Patties* (page 42). It is excellent with spiralized vegetable chips.

✔ Gluten-free   ✔ Wheat-free
✔ Low fat   ✔ Low carb
✔ Paleo   ✔ Dairy-free

Nutrition facts per serving for the dip (50 g):

calories 102 | total carbs 5g | protein 2g | total fat 9g | cholesterol 0mg | sodium 7mg

CHAYOTE AND TROPICAL FRUIT SALSA

Servings 8
Prep time: 5 minutes
Cooking time: 25–30 minutes

Ingredients:

1 chayote or cucumber, diced
1 mango, peeled and diced
1 green chili, seeded and finely chopped
1 cup pineapple, diced
3 scallions, thinly sliced

2 tablespoons fresh mint or cilantro, finely chopped
Juice and zest of 1 lime
Sea salt and freshly ground white pepper, to taste

Directions:

In a bowl, combine all salsa ingredients; season to taste and set aside (may be prepared 2–3 hours in advance and refrigerated until needed).

Serve the pesto sauce with the *Lamb Souvlaki and Rutabaga Rice* (page 138), use in sandwiches and dips, or stir it into cooked spiralized vegetable pasta. Keeps refrigerated for up to 5 days.

✔ Gluten-free ✔ Dairy-free
✔ Paleo ✔ Wheat-free
✔ Low fat ✔ Low carb

Nutrition facts per serving for the salsa (70 g):

calories 30 | total carbs 8g | protein 1g | total fat 0g | cholesterol 0mg | sodium 2mg

BREAKFAST

GOLDEN BEETS, ASPARAGUS, AND SPINACH FRITTATA

Serves 4
Prep Time: 10 minutes
Cook Time: 15 minutes

Ingredients:

*2 medium golden beets, peeled and ends
    trimmed*
1½ tablespoons olive oil
1 leek, white parts only, thinly sliced
2–3 garlic cloves, crushed
1 red bell pepper, seeded and diced
*8 asparagus spears, ends trimmed and
    cut into 1-inch pieces*
2 handfuls baby spinach
*8 eggs, lightly beaten with 2 tablespoons
    non-dairy milk or water*
*Sea salt and freshly ground black pepper, to
    taste*
A dash of cayenne pepper

✔ Gluten-free ✔ Dairy-free
✔ Wheat-free   ✔ Paleo
✔ Low carb   ✔ Low fat

Nutrition facts per serving (237 g):

calories 224 | total carbs 12g |
protein 14g | total fat 14g |
cholesterol 372mg | sodium 175mg

Directions:

Cut two slits lengthwise on opposite sides of the beets (without going through the center), then slice with Blade A.

Heat 1 tablespoon olive oil over medium-high heat in a heavy 10-inch skillet and add the leek. Cook, stirring often, for about 1 to 2 minutes, or until softened. Add garlic, red pepper, and asparagus; cook for 2 minutes. Add beets and spinach and cook for 2–3 minutes longer, until the vegetables are just tender. Don't overcook.

Beat eggs in a bowl, season with salt, pepper, and a dash of cayenne. Pour eggs over the vegetables and cook, gently lifting the mixture with a spatula and tilting the skillet to let the egg run underneath. When the bottom of the frittata has set, turn the heat to low, cover the skillet with a lid, and cook for 5–6 minutes.

Meanwhile, heat the broiler.

Remove lid and place frittata under the broiler for 1–2 minutes to set the top. Remove from oven and let it cool for a few minutes before cutting into wedges and serving.

PERSIAN OVEN OMELET (KUKU)

Serves 4
Prep Time: 15 minutes
Cook Time: 20–30 minutes

Ingredients:

8 large eggs

¼ cup milk of choice

⅓ cup fresh herbs (such as fenugreek leaves, dill, chives, cilantro, and parsley), finely chopped

½ teaspoon turmeric

¼ teaspoon cardamom

A pinch each of cinnamon and nutmeg

Sea salt and freshly ground black pepper, to taste

2 tablespoons ghee or extra virgin coconut oil

1 bunch (5–6) green onions, thinly sliced

3 garlic cloves, pressed

1 large zucchini, spiralized with Blade C

2 handfuls spinach, shredded

Directions:

Preheat oven to 375°F.

In a large bowl, beat together eggs and milk. Stir in the fresh herbs, turmeric, cardamom, and cinnamon and nutmeg, and season to taste; set aside.

Heat ghee or olive oil in a large oven-proof skillet over a medium-high heat; add green onions and garlic and fry gently, for about 2 minutes. Add spiralized zucchini and cook until softened, about 2 minutes. Stir in spinach and cook for 1–2 minutes, until wilted.

Pour the egg and herb mixture over the cooking vegetables; transfer to the oven and bake until the top is nicely browned, about 20 minutes.

Let cool in the pan for about 10 minutes before cutting and serving.

✔ Gluten-free   ✔ Dairy-free   ✔ Wheat-free
✔ Paleo   ✔ Low carb   ✔ Low fat

Nutrition facts per serving (245 g):

calories 232 | total carbs 7g | protein 14g | total fat 17g | cholesterol 389mg | sodium 152mg

SMOKED SALMON, LEEKS, AND CHAYOTE SQUASH OMELET

Serves 4
Prep Time: 15 minutes
Cook Time: 12 minutes

Ingredients:

For the filling:

1 tablespoon butter or extra-virgin olive oil
2 leeks, white and light green parts only,
    chopped
1 orange bell pepper, finely diced
1 garlic clove, minced
1 chayote squash, spiralized with Blade C
A dash of cayenne pepper
¼ cup smoked salmon, flaked
Sea salt and freshly ground black pepper, to
    taste

For the omelet:

1 tablespoon butter or extra-virgin olive oil
4 large eggs
Dash of cayenne pepper
Sea salt and freshly ground black pepper
2 tablespoons chives, finely chopped

Directions:

To prepare the filling, melt butter in a large heavy-bottom or non-stick skillet over medium-high heat; add leeks and cook, stirring frequently, for 3–4 minutes, or until softened. Stir in the bell pepper and garlic and cook for about 1 minute; add the spiralized chayote squash and cayenne and cook for about 2 minutes, until moisture evaporates. Stir in salmon; adjust seasoning to taste and transfer to a plate. Cover with another plate or with aluminum foil to keep warm.

Whisk the eggs and season with cayenne, salt, and pepper. Wipe the skillet with paper towels, add 1 tablespoon butter, and melt over a medium-high heat, swirling to coat the skillet. Pour in the eggs and cook for about 2–3 minutes, tilting the pan and gently pushing the uncooked eggs underneath. Scatter the salmon mixture on top of the omelet, cover with a lid, and continue cooking for 2–3 minutes longer. With a spatula, carefully loosen the omelet and fold in half. Cut into four wedges and serve immediately.

✔ Gluten-free ✔ Dairy-free
✔ Paleo ✔ Wheat-free
✔ Low fat ✔ Low carb
✔ Low calorie

Nutrition facts per serving (210 g):

calories 199 | total carbs 12g | protein 9g | total fat 13g | cholesterol 228mg | sodium 148mg

CREPE PARCELS WITH BROCCOLI STEMS, CARROTS, AND EGGS

Serves 6 (12 parcels)
Prep Time: 15 minutes
Cook Time: 35–40 minutes

Ingredients:

For the crepes:
3 large eggs
1⅓ cups flour
¾ cup milk of choice
1 cup sparkling water
1 tablespoon chives, finely chopped
1 tablespoon extra-virgin olive oil
½ teaspoon sea salt
Extra oil or butter for greasing the pan

For the filling:
2 tablespoons olive oil
1 shallot, finely chopped
1 garlic clove, minced
1 cup button mushrooms, sliced
1 (12-ounce) broccoli stem, trimmed and
*   spiralized with Blade C*
2 medium carrots, trimmed and spiralized
*   with Blade C*
1 handful fresh parsley, finely chopped
⅓ cup shredded cheddar cheese (optional)
10–12 eggs
Sea salt and freshly ground black pepper

Directions:

In a blender, combine all crepe ingredients and blend until very smooth; transfer the batter to a large bowl, cover, and refrigerate for about 30 minutes.

In the meantime, prepare the filling. Heat olive oil in a large skillet over a medium-high heat. Add the shallot, garlic, and mushrooms, and cook until softened and moisture has evaporated, 3–4 minutes.

Add the spiralized broccoli stems and carrots to the skillet and cook for about 3 minutes, until just tender. Stir in the parsley, season to taste, and set aside.

Heat the oven to 375°F.

Lightly brush a 9.5-inch crepe pan (or a non-stick skillet) with olive oil or melted butter and heat it over a medium-high heat. Pour ¼ cup batter into the pan and quickly swirl to cover the pan bottom with the batter. Cook for about 1 minute, until the batter has set, then flip the crepe and cook for further 15 seconds. Transfer the crepe to a plate and repeat, brushing the pan with oil or butter each time until all the batter has been used (yields 10–12 crepes).

Line lightly greased muffin cups with the crepes, letting the edges hang out; add the filling, about ⅔ full. Sprinkle with some grated cheese if using, then crack an egg on top, season, and fold over the crepes to enclose.

Bake for about 15–20 minutes, or until the eggs are cooked to your liking, remove from oven, and let cool for 5 minutes before serving.

Nutrition facts per serving (260 g):

calories 344 | total carbs 28g | protein 18g | total fat 18g | cholesterol 426mg | sodium 177mg

BREAKFAST BURRITO CUPS

Serves 6
Prep Time: 15 minutes
Cooking Time: 15-20 minutes

Ingredients:

6 (8-inch) sprouted grains tortillas

For the filling:
2 tablespoons extra-virgin olive oil, divided
1 small red onion, peeled and sliced with Blade A
1 cup cherry or grape tomatoes, halved
1 jalapeño, seeded and finely chopped
1 garlic clove, minced
1 teaspoon ground cumin

1 (15-ounce) can pinto beans, drained and
     thoroughly rinsed
½ teaspoon Mexican oregano
1 medium zucchini, spiralized with Blade C
6 eggs, beaten
2 handfuls mixed baby greens
4 tablespoons goat cheese or soft cotija cheese,
     crumbled
Sea salt and freshly ground pepper, to taste

Directions:

Preheat the oven to 375°F and lightly grease two 12-cup muffin pans.

Stack tortillas on top of one another and cut into quarters. Line the prepared muffin pans with the tortilla pieces, pressing them down to form cups. Bake for 5 to 6 minutes or until crisp and lightly browned around the edges; remove pans from oven and transfer to a wire rack to cool.

Heat one tablespoon olive oil in a large skillet over a medium-high heat and add the sliced onion; sauté for 2–3 minutes, until translucent. Add tomatoes, jalapeño, garlic, cumin, and beans and cook for 4–5 minutes; stir in the zucchini. Season with salt and pepper and cook, stirring occasionally, for 3–4 minutes, or until the zucchini noodles are just tender.

Heat remaining tablespoon olive oil in a large skillet over medium-low heat. Add the beaten eggs and cook, stirring frequently, for about 4 minutes or until the eggs are cooked to your liking; season with salt and pepper to taste and transfer to a plate.

Divide the bean and zucchini mixture and scrambled eggs between the tortilla cups, sprinkle with cheese and, if you wish, serve topped with the Avocado Sauce (page 2).

✔ Vegetarian ✔ Low fat

Nutrition facts per serving for the cups (240 g):

calories 330 | total carbs 33g | protein 16g | total fat 15g | cholesterol 216mg | sodium 259mg

Nutrition facts per serving for the sauce (20 g):

calories 27 | total carbs 2g | protein 0g | total fat 2g | cholesterol 0mg | sodium 7mg

BUTTERNUT SQUASH, HEMP SEED, AND QUINOA MUFFINS

Serves 12
Prep Time: 15 minutes
Cook Time: 25–30 minutes

Ingredients:

For the muffins:

2 cups butternut squash, spiralized with Blade C
1 egg, lightly beaten
¼ cup raw honey or other sweetener of choice
1½ teaspoons vanilla extract
¼ cup coconut oil
¼ teaspoon sea salt
¼ cup coconut flour
¼ cup hemp seeds
½ teaspoon baking soda
1 teaspoon baking powder
½ cup coconut milk (more if necessary)
1½ cups cooked quinoa

For the topping:

⅓ cup chopped walnuts
2 tablespoons coconut flour
2 tablespoon coconut oil
1 teaspoon lemon zest
3 tablespoons coconut sugar

Directions:

Heat oven to 375°F; grease and line a 12-cup muffin pan with paper cups and set aside.

Place spiralized butternut squash in a blender and pulse a few times until it resembles rice grains.

Add egg, honey, vanilla extract, coconut oil, sea salt, coconut flour, hemp seeds, baking soda, baking powder, and milk, and blend until smooth.

Add quinoa and pulse 2–3 times, until just combined. Scoop batter into the prepared muffin cups.

In a blender or food processor, combine all topping ingredients and pulse until they resemble coarse breadcrumbs. Sprinkle topping over the muffins and place pan in the oven.

Bake for about 25–30 minutes or until a toothpick inserted in the center comes out clean. Transfer to a wire rack and let cool for 10 minutes before removing from the pan.

✔ Gluten-free ✔ Dairy-free
✔ Wheat-free ✔ Low fat
✔ Vegetarian

Nutrition facts per serving (90 g):

calories 210 | total carbs 19g | protein 4g | total fat 14g | cholesterol 18mg | sodium 26mg

CHOCOLATE ZUCCHINI MUFFINS

Serves 12
Prep Time: 15 minutes
Cook Time: 20–25 minutes

Ingredients:

1¼ cup almond flour
¼ teaspoon sea salt
⅓ cup unsweetened cocoa powder
½ teaspoon baking soda
½ cup cornstarch or arrowroot powder
1 teaspoon baking powder
¼ cup tahini
1½ teaspoons of vanilla extract
2 tablespoons coconut oil, melted
⅓ cup applesauce
⅓ cup pure maple syrup (or other sweetener of choice)
1 large zucchini, trimmed and spiralized with Blade C
⅓ cup dark (70% cocoa) chocolate, chopped into small pieces
¼ cup goji berries, soaked in hot water and drained (optional)
¼ cup walnuts, coarsely chopped

Directions:

Preheat oven to 350°F; lightly grease and line a standard 12-cup muffin pan with paper cups.

In a large bowl, mix together almond flour, salt, cocoa powder, baking soda, arrowroot powder, and baking powder.

Place tahini, vanilla, coconut oil, applesauce, and maple syrup in a blender or food processor and blend until smooth. Squeeze moisture from spiralized zucchini and add to the blender; pulse a few times to just combine.

Pour the mixture into the bowl with dry ingredients and whisk gently together; stir in chocolate pieces and goji berries, if using.

Scoop batter into the prepared muffin cups, sprinkle with walnuts, and bake for about 20–25 minutes or until a toothpick inserted in the center comes out clean.

Let muffins cool in the pan for about 15 minutes, before removing carefully and transferring onto a wire rack.

✔ Gluten-free ✔ Vegan
✔ Wheat-free ✔ Low fat

Nutrition facts per serving (70 g):

calories 183 | total carbs 18g | protein 3g | total fat 13g | cholesterol 0mg | sodium 13mg

OVEN APPLE PANCAKE WITH RASPBERRY SAUCE

Serves 6
Prep Time: 15 minutes
Cook Time: 20 minutes

Ingredients:

*1 apple (such as Pink Lady or honeycrisp),
    peeled, cored and spiralized with Blade C*
3 tablespoons grass-fed butter, divided
4 large eggs
⅓ cup raw or brown sugar
1 teaspoon lemon zest
1 cup milk
½ cup heavy cream
1 teaspoon vanilla
¾ cup flour

For the raspberry sauce:

¾ cup raspberries
1 teaspoon lemon juice
2 tablespoons raw sugar or 2 teaspoons honey
¼ cup water

Nutrition facts per serving (180 g):

calories 310 | total carbs 31g
| protein 8g | total fat 18g |
cholesterol 188mg | sodium 75mg

Directions:

Preheat the oven to 425°F.

Melt 1 tablespoon butter in a large saucepan over medium-high heat, add the spiralized apple, and cook until softened; transfer to a plate.

Whisk together the eggs, sugar, and lemon zest until lightened and fluffy. Slowly, stirring continuously, add the milk, heavy cream, vanilla, and remaining 2 tablespoons butter. Whisk in the flour.

Lightly grease a large oven-safe skillet and heat over a medium-high heat. Carefully pour the batter into the hot skillet and let it cook for 2–3 minutes. Top with the spiralized apple and bake for 12–15 minutes, until golden brown.

In the meantime, prepare the sauce. Combine raspberries, lemon juice, sugar, and water in a small saucepan, bring to a boil over medium heat, and cook for about 2–3 minutes, stirring frequently, until the raspberries have softened. Strain through a fine-mesh sieve over a bowl, pressing gently with a spatula; discard the seeds.

Drizzle pancake with the sauce and serve at once.

CRUSTLESS QUICHE WITH CHICKEN, KOHLRABI, AND SWEET POTATO

Serves 8
Prep Time: 15 minutes
Cook Time: 40–45 minutes

Ingredients:

2 tablespoons extra virgin olive oil
1 large red onion, peeled and sliced with Blade A
1 (10-ounces) kohlrabi, trimmed, peeled, and spiralized with Blade C
1 medium sweet potato, trimmed, peeled, and spiralized with Blade C
1 handful kohlrabi leaves or spinach, shredded
1 teaspoons fresh thyme, finely chopped
1 teaspoon fresh oregano, finely chopped
1 cup cooked chicken, diced
6 eggs, lightly beaten
1 cup plain Greek yogurt
½ cup Gorgonzola cheese, crumbled
Sea salt and freshly ground black pepper, to taste

Directions:

Preheat the oven to 375°F. Lightly grease a 9-inch quiche pan or a round baking dish and set aside.

Heat oil in a large sauté pan over medium-high heat, add onion, and cook until translucent, 3–4 minutes.

Add spiralized kohlrabi, sweet potato, kohlrabi leaves, thyme, and oregano and cook, stirring occasionally until softened, 3–4 minutes. Stir in the chicken, season to taste, and remove from heat.

In a large bowl, whisk together eggs and yogurt, add cheese, and season to taste. Stir in the chicken and vegetable mixture and pour into the prepared pan.

Smooth the top and place the quiche in the oven; bake for about 35 minutes, until set and golden brown. Remove from oven and let cool for 10–15 minutes before cutting and serving.

✔ Gluten-free   ✔ Wheat-free

Nutrition facts per serving (200 g):

calories 304 | total carbs 18g | protein 16g | total fat 19g | cholesterol 172mg | sodium 427mg

KOREAN BREAKFAST BOWL

Serves 6
Prep Time: 10 minutes
Cook Time: 25–30 minutes

Ingredients:

3 tablespoons safflower or olive oil, divided
4–5 scallions, sliced into 1-inch pieces
1 red or green chili, seeded and finely
    chopped
2 garlic cloves
1 cup oyster mushrooms, sliced
1 cup broccoli florets, sliced into smaller
    pieces
1 carrot, spiralized with Blade D
1 (12-ounce) Korean or Daikon radish,
    trimmed and spiralized with Blade C
1 packed cup Swiss chard, roughly chopped
1 tablespoon low-sodium soy sauce*
A few dashes of Sriracha, to taste
2 cups cooked brown rice
¼ cup kimchi
6 eggs
Sea salt and freshly ground black pepper, to
    taste
1 avocado, pitted and sliced

*Substitute coconut aminos for a soy-free or
Paleo option.

Directions:

Add 1½ tablespoons oil to a wok or a large heavy-bottom skillet and heat over medium-high heat.

Add scallions, chili, garlic, mushrooms, and broccoli florets and cook, stirring frequently, for 2–3 minutes; stir in the spiralized carrot, radish, and Swiss chard. Cook for 3 minutes further, until vegetables are just tender. Add the soy sauce, brown rice, and a couple of tablespoons of the kimchi juices to the wok and toss to flavor the rice.

Heat the remaining oil in a skillet over medium-high heat; crack eggs into skillet and cook to the desired doneness.

Divide rice and vegetable mixture between six bowls; top each with an egg, kimchi, and avocado slices and serve.

✔ Gluten-free   ✔ Dairy-free   ✔ Vegetarian   ✔ Wheat-free   ✔ Low fat

Nutrition facts per serving (260 g):

calories 276 | total carbs 24g | protein 10g | total fat 16g | cholesterol 211mg | sodium 205mg

STARTERS AND LIGHT MEALS

MUSHROOM AND CELERY ROOT GRATIN WITH HONEY-BALSAMIC VINEGAR REDUCTION

Serves 6
Prep Time: 10 minutes
Cook Time: 45–55 minutes

Ingredients:

For the balsamic reduction:
⅔ cup balsamic vinegar
1½ tablespoon honey
1 sprig fresh marjoram

For the gratin:
½ cup heavy cream
¾ cup half and half
2 sprigs fresh marjoram
1 bay leaf
1½ tablespoons butter

1 leek, white and light green parts only, chopped
2 cups (½ pound) cremini mushrooms, sliced
1 garlic clove, minced
1 small celery root, peeled, trimmed, and sliced with Blade A
⅓ cup grated Muenster or Monterey Jack cheese
2 cups baby arugula, to serve
Kosher salt and freshly grated white pepper, to taste

Directions:

Combine balsamic vinegar, honey, and marjoram in a small saucepan and bring to a simmer over a medium-low heat. Reduce heat to low and let simmer for about 10–12 minutes, until thickened and reduced by half (it should coat the back of a spoon). Remove from heat and transfer to a small bowl.

Preheat oven to 375°F. Lightly grease 6 ramekins and set aside.

In a medium saucepan combine cream, half and half, marjoram, nutmeg, and bay leaf, and bring to a boil over a medium heat. Turn off the heat, cover, and set aside.

In a sauté pan, melt the butter over a medium heat and add leeks; cook until softened, about 4 minutes. Add mushrooms and garlic and cook for 3–4 minutes further, until moisture has evaporated. Season to taste and turn off the heat.

Layer the celery slices into the ramekins, scattering in between mushrooms and grated cheese. Remove bay leaf and marjoram from the cream mixture and slowly pour into the ramekins. Cover with aluminum foil and bake for about 30–40 minutes, until celery root is tender. Remove foil and check with the tip of a knife if the celery root is cooked.

Let gratins cool for 10 minutes in the ramekins. Run a knife around the edges to loosen and turn onto serving plates. Garnish with arugula, drizzle with balsamic reduction, and serve.

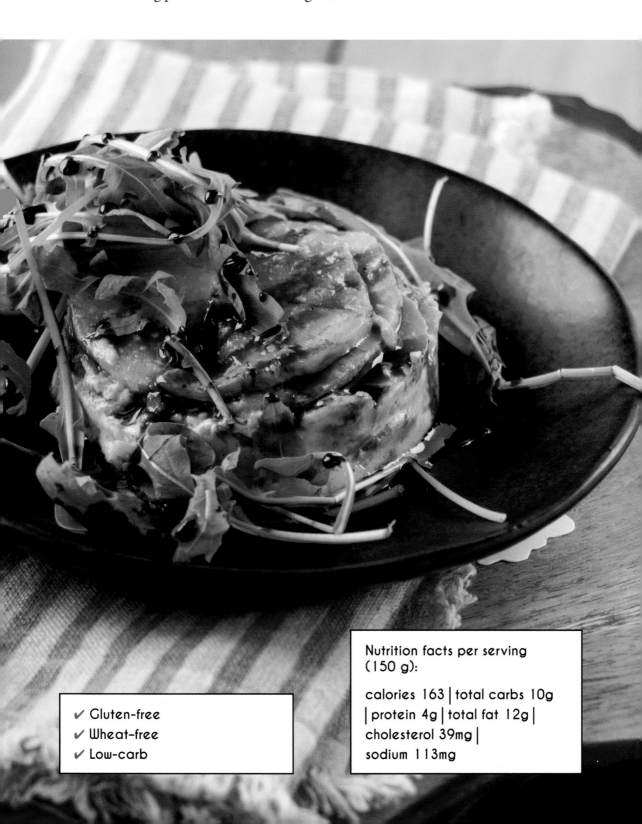

✔ Gluten-free
✔ Wheat-free
✔ Low-carb

Nutrition facts per serving (150 g):

calories 163 | total carbs 10g | protein 4g | total fat 12g | cholesterol 39mg | sodium 113mg

✔ Low fat

Nutrition facts per serving for the tapenade (15 g):

calories 42 | total carbs 1g | protein 0g | total fat 4g | cholesterol 1mg | sodium 102mg

Nutrition facts per serving for the phyllo roll (140 g):

calories 207 | total carbs 16g | protein 8g | total fat 12g | cholesterol 28mg | sodium 275mg

PHYLLO ROLL WITH ZUCCHINI, BRIE, AND OLIVE-ANCHOVY TAPENADE

Serves 4
Prep Time: 15 minutes
CookingTime: 35–40 minutes

Ingredients:

For the tapenade:

¼ cup roasted artichoke hearts, drained
¾ cup Kalamata olives, pitted
¼ cup oil-packed sun-dried tomatoes
2 tablespoons lemon juice
1 teaspoon lemon zest
2 garlic cloves, minced
4 oil-packed anchovy fillets, drained
½ teaspoon dried oregano
1 tablespoons fresh basil
Sea salt and freshly ground black pepper, to
    taste

For the phyllo roll:

1 tablespoon olive oil plus extra for brushing
    the pastry
1 large red onion, peeled, trimmed, and
    sliced with Blade A
1 tablespoon balsamic vinegar
1 medium zucchini, trimmed, and
    spiralized with Blade C
Sea salt and freshly ground black pepper, to
    taste
4 (9 x 14-inch) phyllo pastry sheets*
4 ounces brie, cut into small pieces
¼ cup pine nuts, lightly toasted (optional)

*For gluten-free option, use parchment
paper.

Directions:

Preheat the oven to 375°F. Lightly grease a sheet pan and line with parchment paper.

Place all tapenade ingredients in a food processor and blend to a coarse paste. Season, transfer to a bowl, and set aside.

Heat 1 tablespoon olive oil in a skillet over a medium-high heat, add onion, and sauté until softened and slightly caramelized, about 8–10 minutes. Add balsamic vinegar and spiralized zucchini. Season and cook, stirring occasionally for 2–3 minutes until the zucchini are just tender and moisture has evaporated.

Place one phyllo pastry sheet on work surface and brush lightly with olive oil; place another sheet on top and brush again with oil; repeat with the remaining sheets.

Spread the onion-zucchini mixture in the center of the stacked sheets, about 1½-inch from the edges. Scatter 6 tablespoons tapenade (reserve remaining for another use), cheese pieces, and pine nuts, if using, on top of the zucchini. Fold short side, then sides over the filling and roll up, enclosing the filling completely. Brush with oil and transfer to the prepared baking sheet.

Bake roll until the pastry is golden and crispy, about 20–25 minutes. Cut into 6 slices and serve warm.

CARAMELIZED ONION, RADICCHIO, AND MUSHROOM TARTS

Serves 4
Prep Time: 15 minutes
Cooking Time: 18–25 minutes

Ingredients:

For the pastry:

½ cup coconut flour
⅓ cup tapioca flour
¼ cup coconut oil
½ teaspoon sea salt and a pinch of black
    pepper
1 egg, lightly beaten

For the filling:

1 tablespoon coconut or extra-virgin olive oil
1 large red onion, peeled, trimmed, and
    sliced with Blade A
1 head radicchio, cored and thinly sliced
1 cup mushrooms, sliced
2 sprigs fresh thyme
1 tablespoon balsamic vinegar
1 teaspoon raw honey
⅓ cup coconut cream
¼ cup crumbled blue cheese or goat's cheese
    (optional)
Sea salt and freshly ground black pepper
Baby arugula or micro greens, to serve

✔ Gluten-free   ✔ Wheat-free

Nutrition facts per serving
(200 g):

calories 366 | total carbs 27g
| protein 7g | total fat 27g |
cholesterol 53mg | sodium 66mg

Directions:

Preheat oven to 350°F. Lightly grease 4 (4½-inch) tart pans with removable bottoms and set aside.

Combine coconut and tapioca flours, coconut oil, and salt in a food processor and pulse a few times until it resembles coarse breadcrumbs. Add the egg and pulse until the dough comes together in a ball, adding a splash of water if necessary.

Divide dough into 4 parts and line the prepared tart pans. To blind bake the crust, line with parchment paper and fill with pie weights or dry beans. Bake partially, about 7–8 minutes or until the crust is set, but still pale; transfer to a wire rack and set aside

For the filling, heat oil in a large heavy-bottom skillet over medium-high heat. Add sliced onion and cook until soft and beginning to caramelize. Stir in radicchio, mushrooms, thyme, balsamic vinegar, and honey. Cook, tossing until vegetables are tender, about 3–4 minutes. Season to taste, add cream, and cook for 2 minutes until slightly thickened.

Fill tarts with the filling, scatter cheese on top (if using), and bake for 5–7 minutes, until the pastry edges are golden brown and cheese has melted.

Cool for 5 minutes in the pans before removing; serve garnished with arugula or micro greens.

ZUCCHINI AND WATERCRESS FLAN

Serves 6
Prep Time: 15 minutes
Cook Time: 40–45 minutes

Ingredients:

2 tablespoons extra virgin olive oil
2 shallots, finely chopped
2 garlic cloves, minced
2 medium zucchini, trimmed and sliced
  with Blade A
1 bunch watercress, trimmed and shredded
Sea salt and freshly ground white pepper
¾ cup heavy cream
3 sprigs fresh thyme
3 eggs
2 tablespoons Parmesan cheese, grated
A pinch of nutmeg
A pinch of cayenne

✔ Gluten-free
✔ Wheat-free   ✔ Low carb

Nutrition facts per serving (140 g):

calories 202 | total carbs 4g
| protein 6g | total fat 19g |
cholesterol 148mg |
sodium 57mg

Directions:

Heat the oven to 375°F. Lightly grease a 10 x 7-inch rectangular baking dish and set aside. As the flan will be baked in water bath, have a larger baking pan (such as 15.5 x 10.5 x 2-inches) ready.

Heat olive oil in a large sauté pan over a medium-high heat; add shallots and garlic, and sauté for 1 minute to soften; add sliced zucchini and cook for 2–3 minutes until just tender. Toss in watercress, season to taste, transfer to the prepared baking dish, and set aside.

In a small saucepan, combine heavy cream and thyme sprigs and bring to a boil; turn off the heat and set aside.

Whisk eggs with Parmesan, nutmeg, and cayenne. Remove thyme from the cream and pour slowly into the eggs, whisking constantly. Pour mixture over the zucchini and place the flan dish into the large pan. Pour enough hot water to come ⅔ up the sides of the flan dish and place in the oven.

Bake for about 30–35 minutes, or until set. Remove from the oven and let cool for 10 minutes before removing flan dish from the water bath.

Cool flan to room temperature before serving.

KOHLRABI, CELERY ROOT, AND QUINOA PATTIES WITH CREAMY PEAS AND AVOCADO DIP

Serves 8
Prep Time: 20 minutes
Cook Time: 20–25 minutes

Ingredients:

For the patties:
1 kohlrabi bulb, peeled, trimmed, and
    spiralized with Blade C
1 large carrot, peeled, trimmed, and
    spiralized with Blade C
1 small celery root, peeled, trimmed, and
    spiralized with Blade C
1 cup cooked quinoa
1 green chili, seeded and finely chopped
1 egg, lightly beaten
¼ teaspoon chili powder (more to taste)
1 garlic clove, minced
4–5 scallions, chopped
2–3 tablespoons coconut flour
Kosher salt and black pepper to taste

For the dip:
1 ripe avocado
1 cup frozen peas
1 handful watercress
1 handful dandelion leaves
1 handful arugula
3 tablespoons lemon juice
¼ cup olive oil
3 tablespoons raw pine nuts
2 garlic cloves, crushed
Sea salt and freshly ground black pepper, to taste

Directions:

Preheat oven to 400°F; line a baking sheet with parchment paper and grease lightly; set aside.

Squeeze moisture from spiralized kohlrabi, carrot, and celery root, and place in a blender; pulse a few times to break the noodles into about 1-inch long strands; transfer to a large bowl.

Add remaining patty ingredients (except coconut flour), and mix to combine; add 2–3 tablespoons coconut flour, until the mixture holds together.

Scoop out a ¼ cup of the mixture and shape into a patty; place on the prepared baking sheet. Repeat until all the mixture has been used. Place in the oven and bake for 12–15 minutes; flip carefully, and continue baking for about 10 minutes further or until the patties are nicely browned.

Alternatively, heat 3–4 tablespoons coconut oil in a large skillet and fry the patties over a medium-high until golden.

Place all dip ingredients in a blender or food processor and blend to a smooth puree. Add a little water to adjust thickness.

Serve the patties with the dip on the side.

✔ Gluten-free ✔ Dairy-free Vegetarian ✔ Wheat-free ✔ Low fat Low carb

Nutrition facts per serving for the patties (107 g):

calories 80 | total carbs 13g | protein 4g | total fat 2g | cholesterol 26mg | sodium 67mg

Nutrition facts per serving for the dip (50 g):

calories 102 | total carbs 5g | protein 2g | total fat 9g | cholesterol 0mg | sodium 7mg

KOREAN RADISH-WRAPPED PRAWNS WITH BLACK RICE WAFERS AND CHILI SAUCE

Serves 4
Prep Time: 15–20 minutes
Cook Time: 15 minutes

Ingredients:

For the chili sauce:

2 tablespoons Harissa paste, or hot sauce of
    choice
4 garlic cloves, peeled
2-inch piece fresh ginger, peeled and minced
1 tablespoon coconut aminos
1 teaspoon raw honey
½ cup tomato juice (or more as needed)

For the waffles:

2 cups cooked black rice (1 cup uncooked)
2 eggs
2 teaspoons baking powder
1 tablespoon arrowroot powder
1 teaspoon raw honey
½ cup coconut milk
1 tablespoon coconut oil, melted

For the prawns:

1 medium Korean radish (or Daikon radish),
    peeled and spiralized with Blade D
1 tablespoon fresh Thai basil, finely chopped
1 tablespoon cilantro, finely chopped
1 egg
1 tablespoon coconut milk or water
1 pound (16–20) large prawns, peeled
    (tails-on) and de-veined
⅓ cup arrowroot powder
Sea salt and freshly ground pepper, to taste
Coconut oil for frying

Directions:

Place all of the chili sauce ingredients in a blender and blitz until smooth. Season to taste and set aside.

In a blender or food processor, combine the waffle ingredients and process to a smooth batter, adding a little water if too thick. Cook in a waffle maker according to the manufacturer's instructions (makes 2–3 waffles depending on the model). Cut the waffles in 4 and keep warm.

Gently squeeze the moisture from the spiralized radish, toss with the Thai basil and cilantro, and spread on kitchen paper towels; set aside.

In a small bowl, lightly beat the egg with 1 tablespoon coconut milk or water and place the arrowroot powder in another bowl.

Season the prawns, hold by the tail, and dredge in arrowroot powder, dip into the egg, then wrap tightly with some radish strands and set aside. Repeat with the remaining prawns.

Line a large plate with paper towels and set aside.

In a medium skillet, heat about ½ inch of coconut oil over medium-high heat and fry a few prawns at a time, turning once, until golden brown (about 1–2 minutes per side). Transfer to the paper-lined plate.

Alternatively, place the prawns on a non-stick baking mat and bake at 375°F until golden brown.

Serve prawns with the black rice waffles and chili sauce.

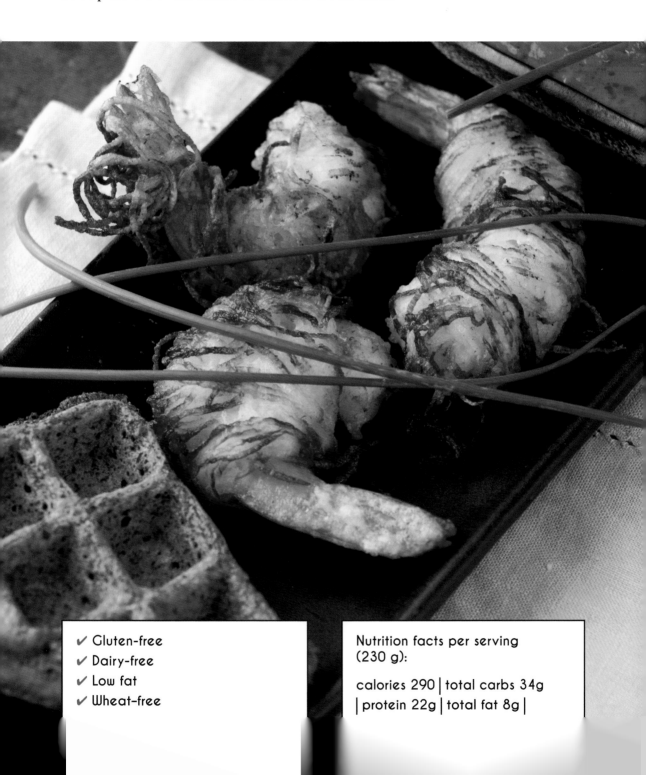

✔ Gluten-free
✔ Dairy-free
✔ Low fat
✔ Wheat-free

Nutrition facts per serving (230 g):

calories 290 | total carbs 34g | protein 22g | total fat 8g |

BUTTERNUT SQUASH, PARSNIP, AND PEA HUMMUS WITH CRUDITÉS

Serves 8
Prep Time: 10–12 minutes
Cook Time: 8–10 minutes

Ingredients:

2 tablespoons extra-virgin olive oil, divided
1 (½-pound) piece butternut squash, peeled and spiralized with Blade C
1 large parsnip, peeled, trimmed, and spiralized with Blade C
1 ½ cup fresh or frozen peas
⅛ cup tahini
1–2 tablespoons lemon juice, to taste
½ teaspoon ground cumin
½ teaspoon ground coriander
¼ teaspoon cayenne pepper or red chili flakes (more to taste)
1–2 garlic cloves, crushed
Sea salt, to taste
A selection of crudités, to serve (broccoli and cauliflower florets, baby carrots, sliced cucumbers, and other vegetables of choice)

✔ Gluten-free ✔ Dairy-free
✔ Wheat-free ✔ Low fat
✔ Low carb

Nutrition facts per serving (90 g):

calories 106 | total carbs 13g
| protein 3g | total fat 6g |
cholesterol 0mg | sodium 9mg

Directions:

Heat olive oil in a large sauté pan over medium heat and add the butternut squash and parsnip noodles; cover with a lid and cook, tossing often, until tender, and begin to caramelize slightly, about 5–7 minutes. Set aside to cool.

Fill a large bowl with water and add a couple handfuls of ice.

In a large saucepan, bring 4 cups water to boil over a high heat; add ¼ teaspoon salt and the peas. Cook for about 2 minutes, until tender; drain and plunge into the ice water. Let cool for 1–2 minutes, then drain well and transfer to a food processor.

Add squash and parsnip noodles to the food processor, followed by the tahini, lemon juice, cumin, coriander, cayenne, and garlic, and process until very smooth. Add a little hot water if too thick. Check seasoning and adjust to taste.

Transfer hummus to a bowl, drizzle with the remaining tablespoon olive oil, and sprinkle with a dash of cayenne pepper. Serve with crudités.

PARSNIP AND RUTABAGA RISOTTO PRIMAVERA

Serves 6
Prep Time: 15 minutes
CookingTime: 12–15 minutes

Ingredients:

*1 rutabaga, peeled, trimmed, and spiralized
with Blade B*
*2 large parsnips, peeled, trimmed, and
spiralized with Blade B*
*1½ tablespoons grass-fed butter
(or coconut oil for vegan)*
1 tablespoon olive oil
3 medium shallots, finely chopped
½ red bell pepper, seeded and finely chopped
2 garlic cloves, minced
¾ cup fresh or frozen shelled fava beans
2 artichoke hearts, thinly sliced
⅓ cup dry white wine
*4–5 asparagus spears, trimmed and cut into
½-inch pieces*
Juice and zest of 1 small lemon
*1–2 cups chicken or vegetable broth
(as needed)*
*⅓ cup mascarpone cheese (or coconut cream
for vegan)*
3 tablespoons chives, finely chopped
*¼ cup Parmesan cheese, grated
(or vegetarian/vegan alternative)*
Sea salt and freshly ground black pepper

Directions:

Place spiralized rutabaga and parsnips in a food processor and pulse a few times until they resemble large rice grains; set aside.

Heat butter and olive oil in a large pan over a medium heat; add shallots, and sauté for 2 minutes until softened. Add red bell pepper, garlic, fava beans, and artichoke hearts and cook for 6–7 minutes, or until tender, stirring occasionally, and adding the wine, a little at a time.

Add asparagus, lemon zest and juice, and spiralized rice. Add ½ cup broth and continue cooking for 3–4 minutes, stirring often, and adding more broth as needed to keep the risotto moist. When the vegetable rice is just tender, stir in the mascarpone or coconut cream, chives, and cheese, and remove from heat; serve at once.

✔ Gluten-free ✔ Paleo ✔ Wheat-free ✔ Low fat

Nutrition facts per serving (250 g):

calories 259 | total carbs 33g | protein 10g | total fat 10g | cholesterol 19mg | sodium 59mg

SHRIMP WITH DAIKON RADISH NOODLES, AND PINEAPPLE AND HONEYDEW MELON BALLS

Serves 6
Prep Time: 15 minutes
Cooking Time: 6–8 minutes

Ingredients:

¼ cup rice wine or sherry
2 tablespoons lime juice
1 tablespoon raw honey
1 teaspoon lime zest
1 garlic clove, minced
1 teaspoon fresh ginger, minced
½ teaspoon red chili pepper flakes, or cayenne
1 tablespoon low sodium soy sauce (or coconut aminos for soy-free option)
1 pound (16–20) shrimp, peeled, and deveined
½ small cantaloupe or honeydew melon, deseeded
¼ small pineapple, cored
2 tablespoons fresh mint, finely chopped
2 tablespoons peanut or olive oil
2 cups baby bok choy, shredded
1 Daikon radish, peeled, trimmed, and spiralized with blade D
Sea salt and freshly ground white pepper, to taste
1 teaspoon arrowroot powder, mixed with 2–3 tablespoons water

Directions:

In a large bowl, whisk together rice wine, lime juice, honey, lime zest, garlic, ginger, chili flakes, and soy sauce; add shrimp and toss to coat. Refrigerate for 10–15 minutes.

Scoop the melon and pineapple flesh using a melon baller. Transfer to a bowl and season with a dash of salt and a few grindings of white pepper, and toss with the mint; set aside.

Heat 1 tablespoon oil in a large heavy bottom skillet over medium-high heat, add shrimp, and stir fry until it curls up, about 3 minutes. Transfer to a plate with a slotted spoon.

Add remaining oil to the skillet, add bok choy, and stir until wilted, 1–2 minutes. Add melon, pineapple balls, and radish. Cook, tossing, for about 2 minutes. Return shrimp to the skillet, season, and pour in the arrowroot and water mixture. Stir briefly until thickened and take off the heat.

Serve immediately.

✔ Gluten-free ✔ Dairy-free ✔ Wheat-free ✔ Low fat

Nutrition facts per serving (160 g):

calories 147 | total carbs 7g | protein 16g | total fat 6g | cholesterol 113mg | sodium 223mg

SALADS

Beet, Orange, and Dandelion Salad with Meyer
Lemon Dressing   52

Steak Salad with Apple, Watercress, and Jicama
with Radish Dressing   54

Squash, Apple, and Asparagus Salad with
Pomegranate Dressing   56

Superfood Salad with Walnut Vinaigrette   58

Moorish Zucchini Salad with Mint-Cucumber Dressing   59

Hot and Sour Mushroom Salad with Radish Noodles
and Lemon-Tangerine Dressing   60

Pear and Persimmon Salad with Orange-Tarragon Dressing 62

Thai Crab Salad   64

Avocado, Jicama, and Apple Salad with Mango-Mint
Dressing   66

Baby Spinach Salad with Mixed Berries, Carrots,
Apples, and Raspberry Vinaigrette   68

BEET, ORANGE, AND DANDELION SALAD WITH MEYER LEMON DRESSING

Serves 4
Prep Time: 10 minutes
Cooking Time: None

Ingredients:

For the salad:

⅓ cup shelled fresh or frozen fava beans
1 tangelo orange, cut into segments
1 Fuyu persimmon, peeled and sliced with
    Blade A*
1 cup dandelion leaves, shredded
1 beet, peeled and spiralized with Blade D
1 large carrot, spiralized with Blade D
*If persimmons are out of season, substitute
    with other fruit such as mango, apple,
    or pear.

For the dressing:

2 tablespoons balsamic vinegar
¼ cup Meyer lemon juice, freshly squeezed
¼ cup extra-virgin olive oil
1 tablespoon lemon juice
A dash of hot sauce (optional)
Sea salt and freshly ground black pepper,
    to taste

To garnish:

2–3 tablespoons slivered almonds, lightly
    toasted

Directions:

Add fava beans and 2 cups water to a large saucepan; bring to a boil over medium-high heat and cook until just tender, about 2 minutes. Drain, transfer to a bowl of ice water and let cool for 1 minute. Drain again, peel the skin, and set aside.

In a large bowl, toss together fava beans, orange segments, persimmon, dandelion leaves, and the spiralized beet and carrot.

In a lidded jar, combine all dressing ingredients and shake until well mixed together. Drizzle the dressing over salad, toss lightly, sprinkle with toasted almonds, and serve immediately.

✔ Vegan ✔ Gluten-free ✔ Dairy-free ✔ Wheat-free ✔ Low fat

Nutrition facts per serving (270 g):

calories 283 | total carbs 43g | protein 8g | total fat 11g | cholesterol 0mg | sodium 83mg

STEAK SALAD WITH APPLE, WATERCRESS, AND JICAMA WITH RADISH DRESSING

Serves 4
Prep Time: 10 minutes
Cooking Time: 5–10 minutes

Ingredients:

For the steak:

2 (1½-inch thick) sirloin steaks
  (about 1–1½ pound)
A splash of olive oil
Sea salt and cracked black pepper, to taste
A splash of balsamic vinegar (optional)
A few drops of Worcestershire sauce
  (optional)

For the dressing:

3 tablespoons extra-virgin olive oil
3 tablespoons tangerine or orange juice
2 tablespoons lime juice
½ teaspoon Dijon mustard
Sea salt and freshly ground black pepper,
  to taste

For the salad:

3 cups baby kale or mesclun salad
1 red apple, cored and sliced with Blade A
  and cut into bite-size pieces
½ jicama, spiralized with Blade B and cut
  into bite-size pieces
1 tangerine, peeled and cut into segments
½ cup blueberries
¼ cup pecans, coarsely chopped and toasted
  lightly (optional)

Directions:

Heat a heavy-duty griddle pan or skillet. Rub the steaks with some oil, season with salt and pepper, and place into the hot pan; cook to the desired doneness. For 1½-inch thick steak the cooking times are as follows: about 2 minutes each side for rare, 3 minutes for medium-rare, and about 4½ minutes for medium. If you wish, when you turn the steaks over, add a splash of balsamic vinegar and a few drops of Worcestershire sauce to the pan.

Transfer the steaks to a plate, tent with aluminum foil, and set aside to rest while you prepare the salad.

Combine all dressing ingredients in a lidded jar and shake until emulsified; adjust seasoning to taste.

Add baby kale, spiralized apple, jicama, tangerine segments, and blueberries, to a large bowl; drizzle with dressing, add pecans, and toss gently.

Slice steak thinly, arrange on top of the salad and serve immediately.

Nutrition facts per serving (330 g):

calories 374 | total carbs 24g | protein 23g | total fat 21g | cholesterol 58mg | sodium 71mg

✔ Gluten-free ✔ Dairy-free
✔ Paleo ✔ Wheat-free

SQUASH, APPLE, AND ASPARAGUS SALAD WITH POMEGRANATE DRESSING

Serves 4
Prep Time: 10 minutes
Cooking Time: 3–4 minutes

Ingredients:

For the salad:

1 bunch broccoli rabe (about 1 pound)
1 Opo squash (or 1 English cucumber), sliced with Blade A and cut into bite-size pieces
1 apple, cored and sliced with Blade A and cut into bite-size pieces
8 stalks young asparagus, trimmed and cut into 1½-inch pieces
⅓ cup pomegranate seeds
¼ cup pine nuts, lightly toasted
⅓ cup Comté or Gouda cheese, diced small (optional)

For the dressing:

¼ cup pomegranate juice
3 tablespoons extra-virgin olive oil
2 tablespoons sherry vinegar
1 teaspoon honey
1 tablespoon fresh mint leaves, finely chopped
Sea salt and freshly ground black pepper

Directions:

Fill a large pot with water, add a teaspoon salt, and bring to a boil over a high heat.

Add a couple of handfuls of ice cubes to a large bowl and fill with water; set aside.

Trim and discard the tough parts of the stem ends and the thicker leaves of broccoli rabe.

Wash thoroughly and add to the boiling water. Cook for about 3–4 minutes, until just tender, drain in a colander and add to the ice water; drain well.

In a large salad bowl combine broccoli, Opo squash, apple, asparagus, and pomegranate seeds and toss together.

Add dressing ingredients to a small bowl and whisk with a fork; season to taste.

Drizzle dressing over salad, sprinkle with pine nuts and cheese, if using; serve immediately.

✔ Gluten-free   ✔ Wheat-free   ✔ Low fat

Nutrition facts per serving (310 g):

calories 231 | total carbs 20g | protein 6g | total fat 16g | cholesterol 0mg | sodium 47mg

SUPERFOOD SALAD WITH WALNUT VINAIGRETTE

Serves 6
Prep Time: 15 minutes
Cooking Time: None if rice is pre-cooked

Ingredients:

For the dressing:
3 tablespoons walnut or extra-virgin olive oil
1 small shallot, chopped
2 tablespoons apple cider vinegar
2 teaspoons chia seeds
2 tablespoons toasted walnuts, chopped
½ teaspoon Dijon mustard
1 teaspoon raw honey
Himalayan pink salt and freshly ground black pepper, to taste

For the salad:
2 cups cooked black (or wild) rice
1 English cucumber, spiralized with Blade C and cut into bite-size pieces
1 large carrot, spiralized with Blade C and cut into bite-size pieces
1 bunch watercress, trimmed and shredded
1 cup baby beet greens (or baby spinach)
¾ cup sprouts (such as sunflower, sweet peas, broccoli, or fenugreek)
2 small tomatoes, diced
⅓ cup walnut halves, toasted

Directions:

Place dressing ingredients in a blender and pulse until smooth, adding a few splashes of water if too thick.

In a large salad bowl, combine cooked rice, cucumber, carrot, watercress, beet greens, sprouts, and tomatoes. Add dressing and toss gently to coat. Adjust seasoning and set salad aside for 15 minutes to allow flavors to blend before serving with toasted walnut halves.

✔ Gluten-free ✔ Dairy-free ✔ Vegan ✔ Wheat-free ✔ Low fat

Nutrition facts per serving (200 g):

calories 322 | total carbs 35g | protein 9g | total fat 19g | cholesterol 0mg | sodium 22mg

MOORISH ZUCCHINI SALAD WITH MINT-CUCUMBER DRESSING

Serves 4
Prep Time: 15 minutes
Cooking Time: 5 minutes

Ingredients:

For the salad:

3 tablespoons extra-virgin olive oil
2 each green and yellow medium zucchini,
    sliced with Blade A
1 medium carrot, sliced with Blade A
1 large clove garlic, finely minced
A pinch of ground cumin
A pinch of smoked paprika
Sea salt and freshly ground black pepper,
    to taste

For the dressing:

1 medium cucumber, peeled and diced
⅓ cup fresh mint leaves, coarsely chopped
1 teaspoon lemon zest
1 large clove garlic, minced
3 tablespoons lemon juice
1 tablespoon extra-virgin olive oil
Sea salt and freshly ground black pepper,
    to taste

To garnish:

¼ cup dried cranberries or raisins, soaked in
    water and drained
⅓ cup pine nuts, lightly toasted

Directions:

Heat olive oil in a large sauté pan over medium-high heat. Add zucchini, carrots, and garlic; sprinkle with cumin and smoked paprika and season lightly with salt and pepper. Cook, stirring occasionally, until just tender, about 3–4 minutes; do not overcook. Transfer to a large salad bowl and set aside to cool to a room temperature.

Place all dressing ingredients in a food processor and pulse until smooth. Adjust seasoning to taste and drizzle over the zucchini and carrot salad. Sprinkle with cranberries and pine nuts and serve.

✔ Gluten-free   ✔ Dairy-free
✔ Paleo   ✔ Wheat-free

Nutrition facts per serving (310 g):

calories 261 | total carbs 19g | protein 4g | total fat 21g | cholesterol 0mg | sodium 41mg

HOT AND SOUR MUSHROOM SALAD WITH RADISH NOODLES AND LEMON-TANGERINE DRESSING

Serves 4
Prep Time: 12 minutes
Cooking Time: 5–7 minutes

Ingredients:

For the dressing:
1 tablespoon lemon juice
Juice of 1 large tangerine (about ¼ cup)
1 garlic clove, minced
3 tablespoons extra virgin olive oil
1 teaspoon fish sauce*
1 teaspoon fresh ginger, minced
1 teaspoon hot chili sauce (more to taste)
Sea salt and freshly ground black pepper,
    to taste

*If following Paleo diet, use a salt-fermented
    brand with no additional ingredients.

For the salad:
1 tablespoon extra-virgin olive oil
½ pound fresh shiitake mushrooms
Sea salt and freshly ground pepper, to taste
1 small Daikon radish, peeled, trimmed,
    and spiralized with Blade D
1 purple radish, peeled, trimmed, and
    spiralized with Blade D
1 medium cucumber, trimmed, and
    spiralized with Blade D
1 romaine lettuce heart, thinly sliced
1 bunch scallions, trimmed and thinly sliced
3 tablespoons cilantro, chopped
1 cup Enoki mushrooms, trimmed

Directions:

Add all dressing ingredients to a small bowl and whisk with a fork until well combined; season to taste and set aside.

Stem the mushrooms and slice the caps (reserve the stems to use in stock or discard).

Heat oil in a skillet over medium-high heat; add the mushrooms and let them cook, without stirring, for 1–2 minutes, until softened. Continue cooking for further 4–5 minutes, stirring occasionally; season lightly and transfer to a large salad bowl.

Add the spiralized radishes, cucumber, lettuce, scallions, cilantro, and Enoki mushrooms to the bowl, drizzle with the dressing, and gently toss together.

Divide among salad bowls and serve at once.

✔ Gluten-free ✔ Dairy-free
✔ Paleo ✔ Wheat-free
✔ Low fat

Nutrition facts per serving (330 g):

calories 263 | total carbs 34g
| protein 6g | total fat 14g |
cholesterol 0mg | sodium 45mg

PEAR AND PERSIMMON SALAD WITH ORANGE-TARRAGON DRESSING

Serves 4
Prep Time: 15 minutes
Cooking Time: 10 minutes

Ingredients:

For the salad:

1 shallot, peeled, trimmed, and sliced with Blade A

1 pear, trimmed and sliced with Blade A, cut into bite-size pieces

2 Fuyu persimmons (or cantaloupe or mango), trimmed, peeled and sliced with Blade A, cut into bite-size pieces

4 cups mixed salad greens

¼ cup prosciutto, thinly sliced and cut into 2–inch ribbons

⅓ cup pecan or walnut halves, toasted and coarsely chopped

¼ cup shaved Parmesan or Pecorino Romano cheese (optional)

For the dressing:

½ cup balsamic vinegar

2 teaspoons honey

2–3 sprigs fresh tarragon

2 tablespoons extra-virgin olive oil

3 tablespoons orange juice

1 teaspoon orange zest

Sea salt and freshly ground black pepper, to taste

Directions:

In a small saucepan heat balsamic vinegar and honey; bring to a boil over a medium heat. Add tarragon and reduce heat to low; simmer until reduced in half, for about 10 minutes. Remove from heat, discard tarragon sprigs, and set aside to cool.

In a large salad bowl, toss together shallot, pear, persimmons, salad greens, prosciutto, and pecans or walnuts.

In a small bowl, whisk together cooled balsamic reduction, olive oil, orange juice, and zest; season to taste and drizzle over salad. Scatter the cheese on top, if using, and serve at once.

✔ Gluten-free ✔ Dairy-free ✔ Wheat-free ✔ Low fat

Nutrition facts per serving (230 g):

calories 239 | total carbs 27g | protein 4g | total fat 14g | cholesterol 5mg | sodium 171mg

THAI CRAB SALAD

Serves 4
Prep Time: 15 minutes
Cooking Time: None

Ingredients:

For the dressing:
2 tablespoons rice vinegar
1 tablespoon raw honey
1 teaspoon fresh ginger, minced
3 tablespoons sesame or peanut oil
1 fresh red chili, seeded and thinly sliced
3 tablespoons orange juice
1 tablespoon hot sauce, such as Sriracha
2 tablespoons peanut butter

For the salad:
1 pound (2 cups) crab meat
2 tablespoons Thai basil, chopped
2 tablespoons cilantro, chopped
2 packed cups baby spinach
4 carrots, spiralized with Blade C and
    strands cut into bite-size pieces
1 small Daikon radish, spiralized with
    Blade C and strands cut to bite-size pieces
1 medium cucumber, spiralized with Blade
    C and strands cut into bite-size pieces

To garnish:
5 scallions, thinly sliced
⅔ cup diced mango or papaya

Directions:

Combine all dressing ingredients in a blender and pulse until smooth, adding a little water if too thick.

In a bowl, combine crab meat, basil, and cilantro with 2 tablespoons dressing.

Add spinach to a large platter or salad bowl and add crab meat, spiralized carrots, Daikon radish, and cucumbers on top.

Garnish with scallions, cilantro, and mango, drizzle with the remaining dressing and serve.

✔ Gluten-free ✔ Dairy-free
✔ Paleo ✔ Wheat-free
✔ Low fat

Nutrition facts per serving (380 g):

calories 331 | total carbs 19g | protein 30g | total fat 16g | cholesterol 85mg | sodium 591mg

AVOCADO, JICAMA, AND APPLE SALAD WITH MANGO-MINT DRESSING

Serves 4
Prep Time: 15 minutes
Cooking Time: None

Ingredients:

For the salad:

2 medium carrots, trimmed and spiralized with Blade D

½ mango, peeled, pitted, and diced

1 jicama, peeled, trimmed, and spiralized with Blade D

1 Granny Smith apple, peeled, cored, and sliced with Blade A

2 cups mixed baby lettuce leaves or shredded lettuce

1 avocado, pitted, peeled and diced

4 tablespoons pumpkin seeds, lightly toasted

For the lime dressing:

¼ cup diced mango

3 tablespoons lime juice

½ jalapeño pepper, seeded and finely chopped

¼ cup fava beans, cooked

2 tablespoons fresh mint, chopped

¼ cup plain Greek yogurt

Sea salt and freshly ground black pepper, to taste

Directions:

Combine all dressing ingredients in a blender and blend until very smooth. Add a splash of water if necessary to get a dressing consistency.

Divide dressing between 4 lidded containers or 4 (1-pint) mason jars. Evenly layer on top of the dressing the carrots, mango, jicama, apple, baby lettuce leaves, and the avocado. Sprinkle with pumpkin seeds and serve or refrigerate for up to 2 days. These are great to take to work!

✔ Gluten-free ✔ Dairy-free ✔ Paleo ✔ Wheat-free ✔ Low fat

Nutrition facts per serving (297 g):

calories 239 | total carbs 34g | protein 7g | total fat 10g | cholesterol 2mg | sodium 40mg

BABY SPINACH SALAD WITH MIXED BERRIES, CARROTS, APPLES, AND RASPBERRY VINAIGRETTE

Serves 4
Prep Time: 15 minutes
Cooking Time: None

Ingredients:

For the salad:
1 cup tri-color quinoa, rinsed and drained
¼ teaspoon salt
2 medium purple carrots, trimmed and spiralized with Blade C
3 packed cups baby spinach
1 Pink Lady apple, cored and sliced with Blade A
½ cup fresh blueberries
½ cup fresh raspberries
¼ cup toasted macadamia nuts, coarsely chopped (optional)

For the dressing:
⅓ cup fresh raspberries
2½ tablespoons macadamia nut oil or extra-virgin olive oil
2 tablespoons lemon juice
1 teaspoon honey
1 teaspoon wholegrain mustard
2 tablespoons balsamic vinegar
2 tablespoons fresh basil, finely chopped (optional)
Sea salt and freshly ground black pepper, to taste

Directions:

Add 2 cups water, quinoa, and salt to a saucepan and bring to a boil over medium-high heat. Reduce heat, cover partially, and simmer for about 15 minutes, until the water is absorbed; fluff with a fork, cover, and set aside to cool.

Place spiralized carrots in the food processor and pulse a few times until they resemble rice.

In a large bowl, toss together cooled quinoa, carrot rice, spinach, apple, and berries.

For the dressing, add raspberries, oil, lemon juice, honey, mustard, and vinegar to a food processor and blend until smooth; strain to remove the raspberry seeds and drizzle over the salad.

Serve immediately.

✔ Gluten-free ✔ Dairy-free
✔ Wheat-free ✔ Low fat

Nutrition facts per serving (270 g):

calories 266 | total carbs 38g | protein 6g | total fat 11g | cholesterol 0mg | sodium 69mg

SOUPS

MEDITERRANEAN FISH SOUP WITH RAINBOW CARROTS AND ALMONDS

Serves 6
Prep Time: 15 minutes
Cooking Time: 25–30 minutes

Ingredients:

2 tablespoons extra-virgin olive oil
1 small yellow onion, peeled and finely
  chopped
1 celery rib, trimmed and thinly cut
2 garlic cloves, peeled and minced
2 ripe tomatoes, peeled and diced
½ cup dry white wine (optional)
4 cups fish or vegetable stock
¼ cup ground blanched almonds
Zest and juice of 1 small orange
1 bunch rainbow carrots, trimmed, peeled
  and spiralized with Blade D
1 pound firm white fish fillets, such as cod,
  snapper, or halibut cut into 1½ inch
  chunks
1 cup baby spinach
Sea salt and freshly ground black pepper
2 tablespoons fresh Italian parsley or fresh
  dill, finely chopped
Lemon wedges, to serve

Directions:

Heat the olive oil in a soup pot over medium-low heat; add the onion and celery and cook, stirring often, until softened, about 6 minutes. Add garlic and tomatoes and continue cooking for 2–3 minutes. Pour in the wine and stock and bring to a simmer.

Add the ground almonds, orange zest, and juice; reduce the heat to low, season, and let simmer uncovered for 15–20 minutes.

Meanwhile, cut the spiralized vegetable noodles into 1½ to 2-inch long strands. Add fish, noodles, and spinach to the pot, season with salt and pepper, and cook for about 5 minutes, or until vegetables and fish are cooked. Adjust the seasoning, stir in the parsley, and turn off the heat.

Ladle soup into bowls and serve with lemon wedges.

✔ Gluten-free ✔ Dairy-free ✔ Wheat-free ✔ Paleo
✔ Low-fat ✔ Low-calorie ✔ Low carb

Nutrition facts per serving (375 g):

calories 195 | total carbs 13g | protein 15g | total fat 9g | cholesterol 31mg | sodium 169mg

ROASTED PEPPER AND SUMMER SQUASH SOUP WITH AVOCADO

Serves 6
Prep Time: 15 minutes
Cooking Time: 25–30 minutes

Ingredients:

2 red or yellow bell peppers
2 summer squashes, trimmed
2½ tablespoons extra-virgin olive oil
1 yellow onion, peeled and sliced with
    Blade A
1 fennel bulb, trimmed and sliced with
    Blade A
1 teaspoon ground cumin
3 garlic cloves, peeled and minced

5 cups chicken or vegetable broth
Kosher salt and freshly ground black pepper
Juice and zest from 1 lime
¼ teaspoon red chili flakes
1 tablespoon fresh dill, finely chopped

To garnish:

1 avocado, pitted and sliced
1 tablespoon fresh chives, finely chopped

Directions:

Turn on the broiler, place the peppers on an aluminum foil-lined baking sheet, and roast for about 15 minutes or until charred all over.

Remove baking sheet from oven and carefully fold the aluminum foil over to wrap the peppers and set aside. When cooled enough to handle, remove the skins and deseed the peppers, then cut into ⅓-inch strips.

Trim the yellow squashes and make incisions lengthwise on two opposite sides, being careful not to cut through the center; slice with Blade A.

Heat the oil in a soup pot over a medium-low heat until it shimmers; add onion and fennel and sauté until softened, 5–6 minutes. Add yellow squash and cook, stirring occasionally, for further 5–6 minutes, or until squash is just tender.

Add cumin and garlic and stir for about 30 seconds, until fragrant. Pour in the broth, season, and bring to a boil then reduce the heat to low and let simmer for about 5 minutes.

Add roasted peppers to the pot together with the lime zest, chili flakes, and dill. Adjust seasoning and simmer for further 5 minutes to allow the flavors to come together.

Cut the avocado in half, scoop out the flesh and slice thinly; drizzle with lime juice.

Serve the soup warm or chilled, garnished with avocado slices and chives.

✔ Gluten-free	✔ Vegan
✔ Wheat-free	✔ Paleo
✔ Low-fat	✔ Low-calorie
✔ Low carb	

Nutrition facts per serving (400 g):

calories 133 | total carbs 13g | protein 7g | total fat 7g | cholesterol 0mg | sodium 102mg

CREAMY ZUCCHINI BLOSSOM SOUP WITH MINT

Serves 6
Prep Time: 15 minutes
Cooking Time: 30 minutes

Ingredients:

2 bunches (3 cups) zucchini blossoms, stems cut off

2 tablespoons extra-virgin olive oil

3 shallots, peeled and finely chopped

1 jalapeño pepper, seeded and finely chopped

1 garlic clove, crushed

6 cups vegetable broth

1 medium sweet potato, peeled and cut into 2-inch chunks

1 medium carrot, spiralized with Blade C and cut into 1½-inch strands

1 medium zucchini, spiralized with Blade C and cut into 1½-inch strands

Kosher salt and freshly ground pepper, to taste

½ cup coconut cream

3 tablespoons fresh mint leaves, finely chopped

Directions:

Gently wash zucchini blossoms and place on paper towels to dry.

Heat the olive oil in a large saucepan or soup pot over medium-low heat. Add the shallots, jalapeño, and garlic and sauté, stirring occasionally, for 4–5 minutes. Pour in the broth and bring to a boil. Add the sweet potato, reduce heat, and let simmer for about 15–20 minutes.

Cut zucchini blossoms into 1-inch strips, add to the pot, and cook for 3–4 minutes, until soft. Puree the soup with an immersion blender (or in batches in a food processor) and return to the pot.

Add carrot and zucchini noodles and bring to a boil over a medium heat. Season with salt and pepper; reduce the heat to low and let simmer for about 5–6 minutes, until the vegetables are tender. Stir in the coconut cream and mint, adjust seasoning, and serve.

✔ Gluten-free   ✔ Vegan   ✔ Wheat-free   ✔ Paleo
✔ Low-fat   ✔ Low-calorie   ✔ Low carb

Nutrition facts per serving (350 g):

calories 158 | total carbs 13g | protein 2g | total fat 12g | cholesterol 0mg | sodium 161mg

COCONUT LIME CHICKEN SOUP WITH DAIKON RADISH NOODLES

Serves 6
Prep Time: 15 minutes
Cooking Time: 25–30 minutes

Ingredients:

2 tablespoons coconut oil, divided
1 pound boneless skinless chicken breast,
    diced
2 shallots, finely chopped
1 lemongrass stalk, finely chopped
1 (1½-inch) piece fresh ginger, grated
1 green chili, seeded and finely chopped
2 garlic cloves, chopped
1 teaspoon fresh turmeric, grated
    (or 1 teaspoon ground)
½ teaspoon ground cumin
2 cups coconut milk
4 cups chicken stock
2 teaspoons fish sauce
1 teaspoon raw or light brown sugar
Zest and juice of 1 lime
Kosher salt and pepper, to taste
1 pound Daikon radish, trimmed, peeled,
    and spiralized with Blade D
2 tablespoons Thai basil, chopped

Directions:

Heat 1 tablespoon coconut oil in a soup pot over medium heat. Add the chicken and sear, stirring occasionally, until golden, about 5–6 minutes. Transfer to a plate and set aside.

Add the remaining 1 tablespoon coconut oil, shallots, lemongrass, ginger, green chili, and garlic to the pot and sauté over medium-low heat until softened and fragrant. Stir in turmeric and cumin, return the chicken to the pot, and pour in the coconut milk and stock.

In a small bowl, mix together fish sauce, sugar, lime juice, and zest and stir into the soup. Bring to a boil, reduce the heat and let simmer for 15–20 minutes, until the chicken is cooked through.

Stir in the radish noodles and cook for 3–4 minutes, until the noodles are just tender.

Sprinkle with chopped Thai basil and serve.

✔ Gluten-free   ✔ Wheat-free
✔ Paleo   ✔ Low-fat
✔ Low-calorie   ✔ Low carb

Nutrition facts per serving (370 g):

calories 172 | total carbs 7g
| protein 20g | total fat 8g |
cholesterol 43mg | sodium 190mg

GREEN GAZPACHO

Serves 4
Prep Time: 15 minutes
Cooking Time: None

Ingredients:

4 cups cold water
1 cup baby arugula
1 cup baby kale
1 shallot, diced
2 garlic cloves, crushed
1 large (about 7-ounces) ripe avocado, pitted
  and flesh scooped out
1 tablespoon raspberry or sherry vinegar
2 tablespoons lemon juice
1 (9-ounces) chayote squash, spiralized with
  Blade D
Sea salt and freshly ground white pepper, to
  taste
1–2 tablespoons extra virgin olive oil

To garnish:

1 jalapeño pepper, seeded and finely chopped
¼ cup heirloom or cherry tomatoes, diced
4 tablespoons pumpkin seeds, lightly toasted
  (optional)

Directions:

In a blender, combine water, arugula, kale, shallot, garlic, and avocado and blend until smooth. Season to taste and add vinegar and lemon juice. Add more water if necessary to adjust the thickness.

Add the spiralized chayote and pulse once to break the noodles.

Transfer gazpacho to a serving bowl or a large container, cover, and chill for a couple of hours in the refrigerator to allow flavors to infuse.

Drizzle with olive oil and garnish with jalapeño, tomatoes, and pumpkin seeds before serving.

✔ Gluten-free   ✔ Vegan   ✔ Wheat-free   ✔ Paleo
✔ Low-fat   ✔ Low-calorie   ✔ Low carb

Nutrition facts per serving (350 g):

calories 109 | total carbs 8g | protein 2g | total fat 9g | cholesterol 0mg | sodium 13mg

MINESTRA WITH FENNEL, CARROT, AND ARUGULA-CASHEW PESTO

Serves 6
Prep Time: 15 minutes
Cooking Time: 15–20 minutes

Ingredients:

For the pesto:
¾ cup frozen peas
2 handfuls baby arugula
¼ cup raw cashews
1 garlic clove
2 tablespoons lime juice
3 tablespoons extra-virgin olive oil
Sea salt and freshly ground pepper, to taste

For the soup:
2 tablespoons extra-virgin olive oil
1 leek, white and pale green part only,
    thinly sliced

1 small fennel bulb, trimmed and sliced
    with Blade A
1 red bell pepper, diced
1 garlic clove, pressed
6 cups vegetable stock
1 medium yellow squash, spiralized with
    Blade C
1 large carrot, spiralized with Blade C
A pinch of nutmeg
Sea salt and freshly ground black pepper,
    to taste

To garnish:
1 handful baby arugula

Directions:

In a small saucepan, cover peas with water and cook for 2–3 minutes. Drain, reserve ¼ cup, and add the rest to a blender or food processor. Add arugula, cashews, garlic, lime juice, and olive oil to the blender and blend to a thick, creamy paste, adding a little water if necessary to get the desired consistency. Season and transfer to a bowl. Refrigerate until needed.

Heat olive oil in a soup pot over a medium heat; add leek, fennel, pepper and garlic and sauté until softened.

Pour in broth and bring to a boil. Reduce heat to low, and let simmer for about 8 to 10 minutes.

Add the yellow squash, carrot, nutmeg, peas, and greens, season, and simmer for 5 to 6 minutes or until the vegetables are tender.

Serve the soup with a dollop of pesto and garnish with a few arugula leaves.

✔ Gluten-free ✔ Vegan
✔ Wheat-free ✔ Paleo
✔ Low-fat ✔ Low-calorie
✔ Low carb

Nutrition facts per serving (400 g):

calories 197 | total carbs 16g
| protein 3g | total fat 14g |
cholesterol 0mg | sodium 174mg

CHILLED CHAYOTE, CUCUMBER, AND HERB YOGURT SOUP

Serves 4
Prep Time: 10 minutes
Cooking Time: None

Ingredients:

3 cups plain yogurt
1 teaspoon honey
1 garlic clove, minced
2 tablespoons fresh chives, finely chopped
1–2 tablespoons lime juice, to taste
2 tablespoons fresh dill, finely chopped
1 chayote, trimmed and spiralized with
  Blade D (or use 1 medium cucumber)
1 cup cold water (more if necessary)
Sea salt and freshly ground white pepper,
  to taste
1 tablespoon raisins
2–3 tablespoons walnuts, lightly toasted and
  coarsely chopped
2–3 scallions, thinly sliced diagonally
1½ tablespoons extra-virgin olive oil

Directions:

In a blender, combine yogurt, honey, garlic, chives, lime juice, and dill and pulse until smooth.

Add spiralized chayote and pulse a few times to just break the noodles. Add enough cold water to get a soup consistency. Season to taste and stir in the raisins.

Serve chilled, sprinkled with walnuts, scallions, and dotted with olive oil.

✔ Gluten-free   ✔ Wheat-free   ✔ Low-fat   ✔ Low-calorie   ✔ Low carb

Nutrition facts per serving (380 g):

calories 214 | total carbs 15g | protein 8g | total fat 15g | cholesterol 24mg | sodium 89mg

SWEET POTATO AND CHICKPEA SOUP WITH HARISSA

Serves 6
Prep Time: 15 minutes
Cooking Time: 25–30 minutes

Ingredients:

2 tablespoons olive oil
1 yellow onion, finely chopped
1 celery stalk, chopped
1 medium carrot, peeled and finely diced
3 garlic cloves, crushed
1 teaspoon ground cumin
½ teaspoon ground caraway seeds
½ teaspoon ground coriander
¼ teaspoon ground cardamom
1 teaspoon harissa sauce
¼ cup tomato sauce
6 cups vegetable stock or water
2 (15-ounce) cans chickpeas, washed and
    drained
1 medium sweet potato, trimmed and
    spiralized with Blade D and cut into
    1½-inch strands
Sea salt and freshly ground black pepper

To garnish:
¼ cup Kalamata olives
¼ cup chopped cilantro

Directions:

Heat olive oil in a large pot over a medium heat, add onion and sauté until translucent, 3–4 minutes. Add celery, carrot, and garlic, and cook until softened, about 3 minutes. Add cumin, caraway seeds, coriander, and cardamom and stir until fragrant, about 30 seconds. Stir in harissa, tomato sauce, then season and add vegetable stock or water.

Bring to a boil, add chickpeas, and cook for about 10 minutes over medium heat. If you prefer a thicker soup, transfer 3–4 ladles to a blender and blend until smooth. Return to the pot, add the sweet potato noodles, and cook for about 5 minutes, until the noodles are tender.

Adjust seasoning and serve garnished with chopped olives and cilantro.

✔ Vegan   ✔ Gluten-free   ✔ Dairy-free
✔ Wheat-free   ✔ Low fat   ✔ Low calorie

Nutrition facts per serving (400 g):

calories 233 | total carbs 34g | protein 8g | total fat 7g | cholesterol 0mg | sodium 215mg

BORSCHT WITH BEETS, CARROTS, AND KOHLRABI

Serves 6
Prep Time: 15 minutes
Cook Time: 20–25 minutes

Ingredients:

1 tablespoon canola or grapeseed oil
1 red onion, peeled and finely chopped
1 celery rib, chopped
2 garlic cloves, crushed
1 teaspoon ground cumin
1 teaspoon ground caraway seeds
⅓ cup diced tomatoes
¾ cup frozen lima beans
6 cups vegetable broth or water
Kosher salt and freshly ground black pepper
*2 tablespoons apple cider vinegar or lemon
    juice*
*1 pound (2 medium) beets, peeled and
    spiralized with Blade C and cut into
    1½-inch strands*
*½ large kohlrabi head, spiralized with
    Blade C and cut into 1½-inch strands*
*1 sweet potato, spiralized with Blade C and
    cut into 1½-inch strands*

To garnish:
2 tablespoons fresh dill, finely chopped
⅓ cup sour cream or plain yogurt (optional)

Directions:

Heat the oil in a large saucepan or a soup pot over medium heat. Add red onion and celery stalk and sauté for 3–4 minutes, until softened; stir in garlic, cumin, and caraway seeds and cook for about 30 seconds, until fragrant.

Add tomatoes and frozen lima beans, season, and pour in the stock and vinegar or lemon juice. Bring to a boil, cover with the lid, and reduce heat to low; simmer, for 10–15 minutes.

Add spiralized beets, kohlrabi, and sweet potatoes, and simmer for about 5 minutes, or until the vegetables are just tender.

Sprinkle with fresh dill and serve with a dollop of sour cream or plain yogurt.

✔ Vegetarian ✔ Gluten-free ✔ Wheat-free ✔ Low fat ✔ Low calorie

Nutrition facts per serving (430 g):

calories 122 | total carbs 22g | protein 3g | total fat 3g | cholesterol 0mg | sodium 219mg

VEGAN SCOTCH BROTH WITH TURNIP AND CARROT RICE

Serves 6
Prep Time: 15 minutes
Cooking Time: 30–35 minutes

Ingredients:

1½ tablespoons rapeseed or vegetable oil
1 yellow onion, peeled and finely chopped
1 celery rib, finely diced
2 leeks (white part only), thinly sliced
6 cups vegetable stock
1 bay leaf
2–3 sprigs fresh thyme
½ cup dried red lentils, rinsed
1 bunch kale, stalks trimmed and cut into
    thin ribbons
1 large carrot, trimmed, peeled, and
    spiralized with Blade C
1 rutabaga, trimmed, peeled, and spiralized
    with Blade C
Sea salt and freshly ground white pepper, to
    taste
2 tablespoons fresh parsley, finely chopped

Directions:

Heat a large saucepan over medium-low heat and add oil, onion, celery, and leeks; let sauté for about 8 to 10 minutes until softened. Add the stock, bay leaf, and thyme sprigs and bring to a boil. Reduce heat to low and let simmer gently for 10 minutes.

Add the red lentils and kale and simmer for further 10–12 minutes. Season with salt and pepper and discard bay leaf and thyme sprigs.

Add spiralized carrot and rutabaga to a food processor and pulse a few times until they resemble rice grains; stir into the soup, and cook for 4–5 minutes, until tender.

Serve soup sprinkled with fresh parsley.

✔ Vegan   ✔ Gluten-free   ✔ Dairy-free
✔ Wheat-free   ✔ Low fat   ✔ Low calorie

Nutrition facts per serving (410 g):

calories 166 | total carbs 27g | protein 6g | total fat 4g | cholesterol 0mg | sodium 179mg

FISH AND SEAFOOD

SWEET POTATO-WRAPPED TILAPIA WITH ORANGE SAUCE

Serves 4
Prep Time: 10 minutes
Cooking Time: 15 minutes

Ingredients:

4 (4–6 ounces each) tilapia fillets
Sea salt and freshly ground black pepper, to
    taste
½ teaspoon ground cumin
2 large sweet potatoes, peeled, trimmed, and
    sliced with Blade A
4 shallots, sliced
2 garlic cloves, thinly sliced
¼ cup almonds, blanched and peeled
1 tablespoon dried cranberries
2 tablespoons olive oil
1 orange, thinly sliced
Sea salt and freshly ground black pepper

For the orange sauce:

2 tablespoons olive oil
1 garlic clove, crushed
½ teaspoon ginger, grated
¾ cup orange juice
1 tablespoon sugar free orange marmalade
3 tablespoons fresh parsley, chopped
Sea salt and freshly ground black pepper

✔ Gluten-free   ✔ Dairy-free
✔ Wheat-free   ✔ Paleo

Directions:

Preheat oven to 400°F. Using paper towels, pat dry tilapia fillets and season with salt, pepper, and cumin; set aside.

Cut 4 (16-inch square) pieces of parchment paper. Arrange slightly overlapping sweet potato slices along the center of each parchment paper piece, place tilapia fillets on top, and cover with the remaining sweet potato slices. Scatter sliced shallots, garlic, almonds, and cranberries, dividing evenly, around the fish and potatoes and drizzle with the olive oil. Season lightly and top with orange slices. Fold the paper in half then fold edges tightly to form parcels. Place on a rimmed baking sheet and bake for about 15 minutes, or until the fish is opaque and fork tender.

Meanwhile, prepare the sauce. Heat olive oil in saucepan over a medium heat. Add garlic and ginger and stir for 30 seconds, until fragrant. Pour in orange juice, add marmalade, season, and bring to a boil; reduce heat and let simmer until the liquid is reduced by half and thickened. Stir in parsley.

Transfer parcels to plates, open carefully, drizzle with the orange sauce and serve.

Nutrition facts per serving (300 g):

calories 375 | total carbs 26g | protein 38g | total fat 14g | cholesterol 84mg | sodium 144mg

VEGGIE LINGUINE WITH CLAMS, SPINACH, AND OLIVES

Serves 4
Prep Time: 10 minutes
Cooking Time: 12–15 minutes

Ingredients:

*1 pound large carrots, peeled, trimmed, and
spiralized with Blade B*

*1 pound large parsnips, peeled, trimmed,
and spiralized with Blade B*

3 tablespoons extra virgin olive oil

2–3 garlic cloves, minced

2 anchovy fillets, chopped

*2 (10-ounces) cans boiled baby clams,
drained*

⅓ cup dry white wine or vegetarian broth

2 packed cups baby spinach

*¼ cup black olives, pitted and roughly
chopped*

Salt and freshly ground black pepper, to taste

2 tablespoons pine nuts, lightly toasted

¼ cup fresh parsley, finely chopped

Directions:

Bring a large pot of salted water to a boil over a high heat. Add spiralized carrots and parsnips and cook for 2–3 minutes, until vegetables are tender but firm; drain and set aside. Heat olive oil in a large skillet over medium heat. Add garlic, anchovies, and clams and stir for 30 seconds, until fragrant. Pour in the wine and cook for 1–2 minutes, then add the carrot and parsnip linguine, baby spinach, and olives. Season to taste with salt and pepper and cook, tossing, for about 3 minutes, until the noodles are tender and the spinach has wilted, adding a splash of water if mixture becomes too dry. Stir in pine nuts, basil, and parsley, and turn off the heat. Serve at once.

✔ Gluten-free   ✔ Paleo   ✔ Wheat-free   ✔ Low fat

Nutrition facts per serving (300 g):

calories 352 | total carbs 29g | protein 22g | total fat 15g | cholesterol 49mg | sodium 312mg

COD WITH ALMOND RELISH AND ZUCCHINI SPAGHETTI

Serves 4
Prep Time: 10 minutes
Cooking Time: 12–15 minutes

Ingredients:

4 (6 ounces each) cod or halibut fillets
Sea salt and freshly ground black pepper
2 tablespoons extra-virgin olive oil plus
    enough to brush the fish
1 lemon, thinly sliced
2 shallots, peeled and finely chopped
1 jalapeño, seeded and finely chopped
2 garlic cloves, minced
2 large zucchini, trimmed and spiralized
    with Blade C
2 tablespoons lemon juice
⅓ cup sliced almonds
3 tablespoons raisins, soaked in water
2 tablespoons fresh basil, thinly sliced

Directions:

Preheat the oven to 400°F and lightly grease a 13 x 9-inch baking dish.

Season the cod fillets with salt and pepper and place in the baking dish. Brush fish with olive oil and arrange lemon slices on top; bake for 12–15 minutes or until the fish is fork tender.

In the meantime, heat 2 tablespoons olive oil in a large skillet over medium-high heat and add shallots, jalapeño, and garlic; cook, stirring for about 2–3 minutes, until softened. Add zucchini and lemon juice and cook, tossing, until just tender, 3–4 minutes; add a splash of water if necessary. Stir in sliced almonds, raisins, and basil, and turn the heat off.

Serve immediately.

✔ Gluten-free   ✔ Dairy-free
✔ Paleo   ✔ Wheat-free
✔ Low fat   ✔ Low carb
✔ High protein

Nutrition facts per serving
(300 g):

calories 287 | total carbs 13g
| protein 33g | total fat 12g |
cholesterol 72mg |
sodium 102mg

YELLOW SQUASH FETTUCCINE WITH SALMON, FENNEL, AND LEMON

Serves 4
Prep Time: 10 minutes
Cooking Time: 25–30 minutes

Ingredients:

For the glaze:

1 tablespoon extra-virgin olive oil
⅔ cup orange juice, freshly squeezed
3 tablespoons fresh lemon juice
2 tablespoons balsamic vinegar
1½ tablespoons orange marmalade or honey
1 teaspoon Worcestershire sauce

For the salmon:

1 red onion, peeled and ends sliced off
1 fennel bulb, ends sliced off

2 garlic cloves, minced
¼ cup sun-dried tomatoes, chopped
2 tablespoons fennel fronds, finely chopped
4 (4–6 ounces each) skinless salmon fillets

For the yellow squash fettuccine:

1 tablespoon extra-virgin olive oil
2 large yellow squash, ends trimmed
*Sea salt and freshly ground black pepper,
  to taste*

Directions:

Preheat oven to 400°F.

In a small saucepan, combine 1 tablespoon olive oil, orange and lemon juices, balsamic vinegar, orange marmalade, and Worcestershire sauce. Bring to a boil over medium-high heat, then reduce the heat to low and let simmer, stirring occasionally, until reduced and syrupy (about 8 to 10 minutes). Season to taste and set aside.

Cut a slit down the sides of the onion and fennel bulbs (taking care not to go through the centers) and then slice using Blade A.

Heat 1 tablespoon olive oil in a large oven-safe sauté pan and add sliced onion and fennel. Cook until softened, about 5 minutes; add garlic and sun-dried tomatoes. Cook for 2 to 3 minutes longer, season to taste, and stir in the fennel fronds. Turn off the heat.

Brush salmon with the glaze and place on top of the vegetables. Drizzle remaining glaze over the vegetables and place the pan in the oven. Bake for about 10 to 12 minutes, until salmon is fork-tender.

While the salmon cooks, spiralize the yellow squash using Blade B.

Heat the remaining 1 tablespoon olive oil in a large sauté pan; add the spiralized squash and sauté until just tender, about 2–3 minutes; do not overcook.

Serve the squash fettuccine with the salmon and fennel.

✔ Gluten-free ✔ Dairy-free
✔ Paleo ✔ Wheat-free
✔ Low fat

Nutrition facts per serving (365 g):

calories 347 | total carbs 19g | protein 31g | total fat 17g | cholesterol 77mg | sodium 123mg

STIR-FRIED SCALLOPS WITH RAINBOW CARROT NOODLES

Serves 4
Prep Time: 10 minutes
Cooking Time: 10 minutes

Ingredients:

1 pound scallops
2 tablespoons coconut oil
2 shallots, peeled and sliced
2 garlic cloves, chopped
1 (1½-inches) piece fresh ginger, minced
1 cup sliced fresh mushrooms, such as
   cremini, oyster, or button
1 red bell pepper, seeded and thinly sliced
1 cup broccoli florets, cut small
2 medium carrots, trimmed, peeled,
   spiralized with Blade C and cut into
   2-inch strands

2 medium zucchini, trimmed, spiralized
   with Blade C, and cut into 2-inch strands
Sea salt and freshly grated black pepper,
   to taste

For the Sauce:

2 teaspoons hot chili sauce or 1 teaspoon red
   pepper flakes
2 tablespoons soy sauce or coconut aminos
1 teaspoon cornstarch or arrowroot powder
2–3 scallions, thinly sliced

Directions:

In a wok or a large heavy-bottom skillet, heat 1 tablespoon coconut oil; add scallops and sear for 1–2 minutes per side until opaque (shouldn't be cooked through). Transfer to a plate and set aside.

In a small bowl, combine chili sauce, coconut aminos, arrowroot powder, and ¼ cup water and set aside.

Add remaining 1 tablespoon oil to the wok and add shallots, garlic, and ginger and cook for 2 minutes, until softened. Add mushrooms, bell pepper, and broccoli, and cook, stirring, until just tender. Add carrots and zucchini, season to taste, and continue cooking for 3–4 minutes further, until the vegetables are just tender.

Return scallops to the wok, pour in the arrowroot mixture, and gently stir with the vegetables for about 2 minutes, until thickened.

✔ Gluten-free ✔ Dairy-free
✔ Paleo   ✔ Wheat-free
✔ Low fat   ✔ Low calorie

Nutrition facts per serving (340 g):

calories 219 | total carbs 15g | protein 22g | total fat 8g | cholesterol 37mg | sodium 490mg

SWISS CHARD-WRAPPED RED MULLET WITH CRISPY BEETS AND ONIONS

Serves 4
Prep Time: 15 minutes
Cooking Time: 20–25 minutes

Ingredients:

2 tablespoons extra-virgin olive oil, divided

2 (about 1½ pounds) whole red snappers, cleaned and gutted

Sea salt and freshly ground black pepper, to taste

2 bunches (10–12 leaves) Swiss chard or beet greens, ribs removed and blanched

2 large golden beets, trimmed, peeled, and spiralized with Blade B and cut into 2-inch strands

2 red onions, peeled, trimmed, and sliced with Blade A

2 tablespoons lemon juice, freshly squeezed

Lemon slices and chopped fresh parsley, to serve

For the stuffing:

¼ cup walnuts, toasted and roughly chopped

2–3 garlic cloves, crushed

½ teaspoon ground cumin

5–6 whole allspice berries, crushed

¼ cup fresh parsley, chopped

½ teaspoon lemon zest

½ cup seedless green grapes

Directions:

Heat the oven to 375°F. Lightly grease two rimmed baking sheets and set aside; place a roasting rack on one of the baking sheets.

For the stuffing, in a small bowl, combine walnuts, garlic, cumin, allspice, parsley, lemon zest, and grapes.

Pat the fish dry with paper towels and, if preferred, remove the head and tail. Season with salt and pepper.

On a work surface, arrange 5–6 overlapping blanched Swiss chard leaves. Lay one red mullet on top of the leaves, spoon half of the stuffing into the cavity, then fold the leaves around it, adding a few more leaves if necessary, to completely wrap the body. Brush with ½ tablespoon olive oil and transfer to the baking sheet fit with a rack. Repeat with the other red mullet. Bake for 20–25 minutes, until fish is fork tender.

In a large bowl, combine beets, onions, and 1½ tablespoons olive oil; season with salt and pepper and spread evenly on the other baking sheets.

Bake beets and onions for 20–25 minutes, tossing often, until beets are crispy and onions begin to caramelize.

If both baking sheets fit in the oven, place them side by side and bake fish and beets together for about 20–25 minutes.

Serve immediately, garnished with lemon slices and chopped fresh parsley.

| ✔ Gluten-free | ✔ Dairy-free | ✔ Paleo |
| ✔ Wheat-free | ✔ Low fat | ✔ High protein |

Nutrition facts per serving (340 g):

calories 297 | total carbs 19g | protein 27g | total fat 13g | cholesterol 41mg | sodium 276mg

STEAMED THAI FISH PARCELS WITH VEGETABLE RICE

Serves 4
Prep Time: 15 minutes
Cooking Time: 14–16 minutes

Ingredients:

For the fish:

4 (6-ounces each) white fish fillets (such as
    plaice, cod, pollock, or haddock)
Sea salt and freshly ground black pepper,
    to taste
2 tablespoons lime juice
4 banana leaves, large enough to wrap the
    fish fillets
2 lemongrass stalks (soft inner part only),
    finely chopped
1 (1½-inch) piece fresh ginger, peeled and
    finely chopped
1 small garlic clove, chopped
1 teaspoon lime zest
1 small red chili, seeded and finely chopped
3 tablespoons cilantro or Thai basil, chopped

For the rice:

1 (1-pound) Opo squash, trimmed, peeled,
    and spiralized with Blade B
1 (1-pound) Daikon radish, trimmed,
    peeled and spiralized with Blade B
2 tablespoons coconut oil
1 garlic clove, minced
4 baby bok choy, thickly sliced
2 tablespoons coconut aminos
¼-½ cup coconut milk, as needed
½ teaspoon jasmine flavoring essence
    or orange blossom water (omit if not
    available)
Sea salt and freshly ground black pepper,
    to taste

To serve:

1–2 teaspoons sesame oil
2–3 scallions, thinly sliced diagonally

Directions:

Season fish fillets and drizzle with lime juice; place one fillet in the center of each banana leaf. Alternatively, use parchment paper and/or aluminum foil.

In a bowl, combine lemongrass, ginger, garlic, lime zest, red chili, and cilantro and scatter the mixture evenly over the fish. Fold banana leaves to form parcels and arrange in a single layer, seam side up, in a steamer; cover with a lid and steam for 14–16 minutes, or until the fish is opaque and fork tender.

Meanwhile, place the Opo squash and Daikon radish noodles into a food processor and pulse until they resemble rice grains; squeeze to remove excess moisture, and set aside.

In a large skillet, heat coconut oil over a medium-high heat; add garlic and bok choy and stir for about 2 minutes. Stir in vegetable rice and coconut aminos, and season to taste. Cook, stirring frequently, until the rice is just tender, about 3–5 minutes. Add splashes of coconut milk during the cooking process if the mixture becomes too dry. Stir in the jasmine flavoring essence and fluff with a fork.

Carefully unwrap the parcels and transfer the fish to plates; drizzle with sesame oil and sprinkle with chopped scallions. Spoon vegetable rice alongside the fish and serve immediately.

✔ Gluten-free ✔ Dairy-free ✔ Paleo ✔ Wheat-free ✔ Low fat

Nutrition facts per serving (395 g):

calories 272 | total carbs 9g | protein 30g | total fat 13g | cholesterol 69mg | sodium 171mg

CELERY ROOT, YAM, AND SALMON CAKES

Serves 4
Prep Time: 15 minutes
Cooking Time: 25–30 minutes

Ingredients:

For the salmon:

1 pound salmon fillets
1 bay leaf
4–5 whole allspice berries
3 lemon slices
3 garlic cloves
½ cup white wine (optional)
1 tablespoon extra-virgin olive oil

For the cakes:

2 tablespoons extra-virgin olive oil
2 garlic cloves, minced
1 teaspoon fresh ginger, minced
1 jalapeño, seeded and finely chopped

1 small yam, peeled, trimmed, and
* spiralized with Blade C*
1 small celery root, peeled, trimmed, and
* spiralized with Blade C*
½ teaspoon ground turmeric
½ teaspoon ground cumin
1 egg, lightly beaten
Juice and zest of 1 lemon, to taste
3 tablespoons fresh dill, finely chopped
¼- ½ cup almond flour or panko
* breadcrumbs, plus more as needed to coat*
Sea salt and freshly ground black pepper,
* to taste*

Directions:

Preheat the oven to 375°F; line a baking sheet with parchment paper and set aside.

Place salmon fillets in a large saucepan and add bay leaf, allspice berries, lemon, garlic, and wine, if using. Pour in enough water to just cover the salmon and bring to a boil, then reduce heat and simmer for about 5–6 minutes, or until the salmon is opaque. Transfer salmon with a slotted spoon to a large bowl, remove skin, if any, and flake with a fork; set aside. Alternatively, skip this step and use 2 (15-ounce) cans salmon.

In a large skillet, heat olive oil over a medium-high heat. Add garlic, ginger, and jalapeño and stir for 30 seconds. Add spiralized yam and celery root, and cook, tossing often, for about 4–5 minutes, or until tender. Add to the salmon, along with the turmeric, cumin, egg, lemon juice and zest; season to taste and mix to combine, adding a little almond flour at a time if too wet.

Scooping about ¼ cup of the mixture at a time, form into 1-inch thick, about 3-inch in diameter patties. If you have the time, refrigerate for up to 30 minutes. Roll the cakes in almond flour, pressing lightly, and place on the prepared baking sheet. Bake for about 15 minutes, flipping them over once, or until crispy and golden brown. Alternatively, in a large skillet, heat 2–3 tablespoons olive oil or butter and fry the cakes, flipping over once, until golden brown, about 4–5 minutes.

Serve salmon cakes with a salad of choice.

✔ Gluten-free ✔ Dairy-free
✔ Paleo ✔ Wheat-free
✔ High Protein

Nutrition facts per serving (380 g):

calories 398 | total carbs 19g | protein 28g | total fat 23g | cholesterol 114mg | sodium 118mg

MASALA SCALLOPS WITH RUTABAGA RICE

Serves 4
Prep Time: 10 minutes
Cooking Time: 15 minutes

Ingredients:

For the rice:

2 rutabagas, peeled, trimmed, and spiralized
    with Blade C
1 tablespoon coconut oil
2 tablespoons scallions, chopped
Sea salt and freshly ground black pepper,
    to taste

For the masala sauce:

½ tablespoon coconut oil
1 red onion, peeled, trimmed, and sliced
    with Blade A
½ teaspoon mustard seeds
1 (2-inch) piece ginger, minced
2–3 garlic cloves, minced
1 green chili, seeded and finely chopped
1 large tomato, peeled and diced
1 teaspoon garam masala
⅔ cup frozen peas
Sea salt and freshly ground black pepper,
    to taste
½ cup coconut cream

For the scallops:

1 pound (15–20) scallops
1½ tablespoon coconut oil
1–2 tablespoons freshly squeezed lemon juice
2 tablespoons cilantro, finely chopped, to
    garnish

Directions:

Place spiralized rutabagas in a food processor and pulse until they resemble rice grains.

Heat 1 tablespoon coconut oil in a large skillet over a medium-high heat, add scallions and rutabaga rice, season to taste and cook, tossing occasionally for 3–5 minutes or until just tender.

Heat coconut oil in a large saucepan and add onion; sauté, stirring occasionally, until softened, about 3–4 minutes. Add mustard seeds, ginger, garlic, and chili, and cook, stirring often until fragrant, about 2 minutes. Stir in tomato, garam masala, peas, and 1 cup water; season to taste and cook for 3–5 minutes.

In the meantime, pat dry scallops with kitchen paper towels. Heat coconut oil in a large heavy-bottom skillet over high heat and fry scallops, flipping once, for about 1½–2 minutes per side; do not overcook).

Stir coconut cream into the sauce and bring to a simmer; add scallops and cilantro and let simmer for about 1 minute.

Spoon scallops and sauce over the rutabaga rice and serve immediately.

✔ Gluten-free ✔ Dairy-free
✔ Paleo   ✔ Wheat-free

Nutrition facts per serving (345 g):

calories 358 | total carbs 20g | protein 23g | total fat 22g | cholesterol 37mg | sodium 205mg

INDONESIAN SHRIMP CURRY WITH JEWELED DAIKON RADISH RICE

Serves 4
Prep Time: 20 minutes
Cooking Time: 30 minutes

Ingredients:

For the curry:

2 tablespoons coconut oil

1 onion, peeled, trimmed, and sliced with Blade A

2 garlic cloves, thinly sliced

2 lemongrass stalks, white part only, finely chopped

1 (1-inch) piece fresh ginger, finely grated

1 red chili, seeded and thinly sliced

1 Asian eggplant, peeled, trimmed, and sliced with Blade A

2 teaspoons curry powder, mixed to a paste with 2–3 tablespoons water

2 teaspoons tamarind paste, mixed with 1½ cups water

⅓ cup coconut milk

1 pound shrimp, peeled and deveined

Sea salt and freshly ground black pepper, to taste

For the Jeweled Rice:

2 medium turnips, peeled, trimmed, and spiralized with Blade C

2 medium carrots, peeled, trimmed, and spiralized with Blade C

2 tablespoons extra virgin olive oil

½ each red, yellow, and green bell peppers, seeded and finely chopped

¼ teaspoon of each ground cardamom and ground cumin

1 teaspoon orange zest

¼ cup shredded coconut (optional)

¼ cup dried raisins (optional)

⅓ cup freshly squeezed orange juice

Sea salt and freshly ground black pepper

To serve:

2–3 tablespoons slivered almonds

2–3 tablespoons Thai basil, shredded

½ cup fresh pineapple chunks (optional)

Directions:

For the jeweled rice, place spiralized turnips and carrots in a food processor and pulse until they resemble rice grains.

Heat olive oil in a large skillet and add the bell peppers and cook, stirring often, until softened. Add spices and stir for 30 seconds, until fragrant, then add spiralized rice, orange zest, shredded coconut, and raisins, if using. Season to taste; add orange juice and cook, tossing often, until rice is tender, about 4–5 minutes. Add a splash of water if the mixture becomes too dry. Set aside.

Heat coconut oil in a large pan, add onion, and sauté for 4–5 minutes until translucent. Add garlic, lemongrass, and ginger, and cook for 1–2 minutes, then add spiralized eggplant. Continue cooking, tossing occasionally, for 3–4 minutes. Stir in the curry powder and pour in the tamarind water and coconut cream; season to taste and bring to a boil. Reduce the heat and let simmer for about 10 minutes, or until the eggplant is cooked. Add the shrimp and cook for about 5–6 minutes.

Serve the curry immediately over the turnip and carrot rice and garnish with slivered almonds, Thai basil, and pineapple chunks, if desired.

✔ Gluten-free   ✔ Dairy-free
✔ Paleo   ✔ Wheat-free
✔ Low fat

Nutrition facts per serving (410 g):

calories 353 | total carbs 22g | protein 26g | total fat 19g | cholesterol 170mg | sodium 240mg

POULTRY

CITRUS CHICKEN WITH RATATOUILLE TIMBALES

A timbale is a French term, derived from "Timballo," which is a type of drum.

Serves 6
Prep Time:25 minutes
Cooking Time: 1 hour

Ingredients:

For the chicken:

2 tablespoons extra-virgin olive oil
4 (6 ounces each) boneless skinless chicken
*   breasts, cut into 1½-inch pieces*
2 shallots, finely chopped
3 garlic cloves, minced
2 teaspoons paprika
1 cup low-sodium chicken broth
1 teaspoon raw honey
Zest and juice of 1 lemon
1 fresh bay leaf
2 fresh thyme sprigs
1 teaspoon Dijon mustard
Zest and juice of 1 orange
Kosher salt and freshly ground black pepper,
*   to taste*

For the timbales:

1½ tablespoons extra-virgin olive oil
1 medium yellow onion, peeled, trimmed,
*   and sliced with Blade A*
2 garlic cloves, minced
1 small eggplant, peeled and diced
1 jalapeño pepper, seeded and diced
1 each green and red bell pepper, seeded
*   and diced*
2 ripe medium tomatoes, grated
½ teaspoon Herbs de Provence or dried thyme
2 medium zucchini, trimmed and spiralized
*   with Blade C*
1 large carrot, spiralized with Blade C
2–3 tablespoons pitted olives (optional)
2 eggs, lightly beaten with 1 tablespoon milk
*   of choice*
Sea salt and freshly ground black pepper

Directions:

Preheat oven to 400°F.

Heat oil in a large heavy-bottom skillet over a medium-high heat; add chicken and sear, turning often, until lightly browned all over. Add shallots and garlic, and cook for 2 minutes until softened; stir in paprika and pour in chicken broth. Bring to a boil; add honey, lemon zest and juice, bay leaf, thyme sprigs, mustard, and orange zest and juice. Reduce heat to low, cover with a lid and let simmer until chicken is cooked though and the sauce is reduced, about 20 minutes.

For the ratatouille timbales, preheat the oven to 375°F and lightly grease 6 ramekins.

Heat the olive oil in a large skillet over medium- high heat. Add the onion and sauté until translucent, 5–6 minutes. Add garlic, eggplant, jalapeño, and bell peppers, and cook, stirring occasionally until tender, about 5 minutes. Add tomatoes and herbs and cook until the sauce has thickened, 5–6 minutes. Stir in the spiralized zucchini and carrot and cook, tossing, for 3–4 minutes, until tender. Transfer ratatouille to a large bowl and mix in the eggs.

Divide the mixture between the prepared ramekins, pressing down with a ½-cup measuring cup.

Place in the oven and bake until the top is golden brown, about 15–20 minutes. Transfer to a wire rack and let stand for 5 minutes, before running a knife around the edge and turning the timbales onto plates. Add chicken and serve with the pepper sauce.

✔ Gluten-free ✔ Dairy-free
✔ Wheat-free ✔ Low fat
✔ High protein ✔ Low carb
✔ Paleo

Nutrition facts per serving (375 g):

calories 296 | total carbs 17g | protein 31g | total fat 12g | cholesterol 135mg | sodium 155mg

OVEN-BAKED TURKEY KEFTEDES WITH CARROT AND BEET SALAD

Keftedes are Greek meatballs.

Serves 4
Prep Time: 15 minutes
Cooking Time: 25–30 minutes

Ingredients:

For the keftedes:

1 small red onion, grated and excess
   juices drained
1 green chili, seeded and finely chopped
2 garlic cloves, minced
1½ pound lean ground turkey
1 egg, lightly beaten
¼ teaspoon cinnamon
⅛ teaspoon nutmeg
1 teaspoon ground cumin
½ teaspoon ground coriander
1 tablespoon fresh oregano, chopped
1 tablespoon fresh mint leaves, finely chopped
1 tablespoon extra-virgin olive oil
¼ cup almond flour (more as needed)
Sea salt and freshly ground black pepper,
   to taste
Extra-virgin olive oil, for brushing

For the salad:

4 spring onions, finely chopped
2 tablespoons fresh parsley, finely chopped
½ teaspoon raw honey
Juice and zest of 1 small lemon
3 tablespoons pitted Kalamata olives,
   chopped
3 tablespoons extra-virgin olive oil
2 large carrots, peeled, trimmed, and
   spiralized with Blade C
2 medium beets, peeled, trimmed, and
   spiralized with Blade C
Sea salt and freshly ground black pepper, to
   taste
⅓ cup feta cheese, crumbled (optional)

Directions:

Preheat the oven to 375°F; line a rimmed baking sheet with silicon baking mat or aluminum foil (if using aluminum foil, cover it with parchment paper).

In a large mixing bowl, combine all of the ingredients for keftedes and mix well. You may refrigerate the mixture for 1–2 hours to allow the flavors to blend.

Scoop a heaped tablespoon of the mixture and roll into a ball or oval shape; place on the prepared baking sheet and repeat until all the mixture is used, spacing the keftedes about an inch apart. Brush keftedes with olive oil and bake until nicely browned, about 25–30 minutes, turning over midway through the cooking time.

In a large bowl, whisk together spring onions, parsley, honey, lemon juice and zest, olives, and olive oil. Add spiralized beets and carrots; toss together to coat. Sprinkle crumbled feta cheese on top, if using, and serve salad with the keftedes.

✔ Gluten-free ✔ Wheat-free
✔ Low carb ✔ High Protein

Nutrition facts per serving
(330 g):

calories 437 | total carbs 14g
| protein 34g | total fat 27g
| cholesterol 187mg | sodium
326mg

PINE NUT AND MUSHROOM-STUFFED CHICKEN BREASTS WITH ZUCCHINI SPAGHETTI

Serves 4
Prep Time: 20 minutes
Cook Time: 15–20 minutes

Ingredients:

For the chicken:

1½ tablespoons extra-virgin olive oil (or melted grass-fed butter or ghee)

1 leek, white parts only, thinly sliced

2 cups (6-ounces) cremini mushrooms, thinly sliced

4 tablespoons sun-dried tomatoes, drained and chopped

1 teaspoon fresh thyme, chopped

2 garlic cloves, minced

2 tablespoons fresh parsley, finely chopped

½ cup fresh mozzarella or burrata cheese, diced small

2 tablespoon pine nuts, lightly toasted

4 (5–6 ounces each) boneless skinless chicken breasts

Sea salt and freshly ground black pepper, to taste

1 tablespoon extra-virgin olive oil

¼ cup balsamic vinegar

¾ cup low sodium chicken stock

1–2 tablespoons mascarpone cheese

For the spaghetti:

1 tablespoon extra-virgin olive oil

1 garlic clove, minced

1 pound (3 medium) zucchini, trimmed, and spiralized with Blade C

2 tablespoons fresh basil leaves, thinly sliced

Directions:

For the stuffing, heat 1 tablespoon olive oil in a large skillet over a medium-high heat; add leeks and sauté until softened, 3–4 minutes. Add mushrooms and cook until tender and most of the moisture has evaporated, 7–8 minutes. Transfer leeks and mushrooms to a small bowl and add the sundried tomatoes, thyme, garlic, parsley, mozzarella, and pine nuts; season to taste and toss together.

Preheat the oven to 375°F.

Pat-dry the chicken breasts and place one on a cutting board. Cut a slit along the thick side of the breast, without going all the way through. Open the breast, cover loosely with plastic food wrap and pound it with a meat mallet or a rolling pin until evenly flattened to about ¼-inch thickness. Spoon 1–2 tablespoons of the stuffing in the center of the breast and roll it up, tucking in the ends; secure with kitchen twine or wooden toothpicks. Repeat with the remaining breasts. Reserve any remaining stuffing.

Heat olive oil in a large oven-safe skillet over a medium-high heat; add the rolls, seamed side down, and sear on all sides until browned. Add balsamic vinegar and chicken stock to the skillet; reduce the heat to low and cover with a lid. Cook for 3–4 minutes, then transfer the skillet to the oven and cook for about 20–25 minutes, removing the lid midway through.

Carefully remove skillet from the oven and transfer the rolls to a plate; tent with aluminum foil and set aside. Stir 1–2 tablespoons mascarpone cheese into the skillet juices to thicken.

For the spaghetti, heat olive oil in a large skillet over a medium-high heat; add garlic and spiralized zucchini and cook, tossing, until just tender, about 3–4 minutes. Add any remaining stuffing and basil leaves, continue cooking for further 2–3 minutes, and remove from the heat.

Remove twine or toothpicks and slice the chicken rolls. Serve with the zucchini spaghetti and drizzle with the sauce.

✔ Gluten-free ✔ Wheat-free
✔ Low carb ✔ High protein

Nutrition facts per serving (350 g):

calories 379 | total carbs 11g | protein 39g | total fat 20g | cholesterol 97mg | sodium 227mg

YAKITORI CHICKEN WITH YOUNG COCONUT AND DAIKON SALAD

Serves 4
Prep Time: 25 minutes
Cooking Time: 12–15 minutes

Ingredients:

1½ pounds boneless, skinless chicken thighs, cut into 1½-inch pieces

8 large spring onions, white part only, cut into 1½-inch pieces

10–12 (6-inch) wooden skewers, soaked in water for 1–2 hours

2 teaspoons Japanese 7-spice blend (shichimi togarashi), optional

For the yakitori sauce:

½ cup mirin

1 (1½-inch) piece fresh ginger, peeled and chopped

⅓ cup sake

2–3 garlic cloves, crushed

2 tablespoons canola or other neutral-tasting oil

2 tablespoons rice vinegar

½ cup low sodium soy sauce

A few dashes Sriracha chili sauce, to taste

2 tablespoons brown sugar

Coarsely ground black pepper, to taste

For the salad:

1 Thai young coconut

1 tablespoon lime juice

2 packed cups young mustard greens or mesclun salad

1 medium Daikon radish, peeled, trimmed, and spiralized with Blade D

1 broccoli stalk, trimmed, and spiralized with Blade D

1 large carrot, peeled, trimmed, and spiralized with Blade D

1 mango, peeled, pitted, and julienned

3 scallions, trimmed and thinly sliced

For the dressing:

2 tablespoons low sodium soy sauce

1 tablespoon rice vinegar

1 tablespoon ume plum vinegar or red wine vinegar

1 tablespoon sesame or vegetable oil

1 teaspoon raw honey or sugar

1 teaspoon lime zest

A few dashes Sriracha chili sauce, to taste

To garnish: (optional)

Dried bonito flakes

Toasted seaweed, thinly sliced

2 tablespoons sesame seeds, toasted

Directions:

Combine all sauce ingredients in a small saucepan and bring to a boil over medium–high heat. Reduce heat to low and let simmer until slightly thickened, about 4–5 minutes; set aside and let cool.

Place chicken pieces in a large resealable plastic bag and add about ½ cup of the sauce; mix well to coat the chicken and refrigerate for 1–2 hours. Pour about ¼ cup of the sauce in a small bowl for basting the chicken skewers and reserve the remaining.

Thread chicken onto the soaked skewers, alternating 2 chicken pieces with 1 spring onion piece.

For the salad, open the coconut top and scoop out the meat. Cut coconut meat into thin strips and drizzle with lime juice; add to a large bowl and toss together with the remaining salad ingredients.

Lightly spray a grill pan (cast iron, preferably) with a cooking oil spray and heat over a medium-high heat. Working in batches, grill the chicken skewers, turning them often and basting with the sauce, until cooked through and browned, about 7–8 minutes. Transfer to a plate and tent with aluminum foil to keep warm.

In a small bowl, combine all dressing ingredients and whisk with a fork; drizzle over the salad and toss. Top with desired garnishes, if using.

Sprinkle skewers with the 7-blend spice and serve with the salad and the remaining yakitori sauce on the side.

✔ Dairy-free   ✔ Low fat   ✔ Low carb   ✔ High protein

Nutrition facts per serving (360 g):

calories 331 | total carbs 16g | protein 36g | total fat 14g | cholesterol 139mg | sodium 454mg

Nutrition facts per serving for the sauce (20 g):

calories 34 | total carbs 4g | protein 0g | total fat 1g | cholesterol 0mg | sodium 265mg

CHERMOULA CHICKEN WITH TARO, CARROT, AND RUTABAGA PASTA

Chermoula is a Moroccan herb paste.

Serves 4-6
Prep Time: 20 minutes
Cook Time: 45-50 minutes

Ingredients:

Chermoula paste:

⅓ cup extra virgin olive oil

3 tablespoons each fresh flat-leaf parsley and cilantro

2–3 garlic cloves, minced

1 (1-inch piece) fresh ginger

1½ teaspoons paprika

1 teaspoon ground coriander

½ teaspoon smoked paprika

½ teaspoon red chili pepper flakes

1 teaspoon ground cumin

2 tablespoons lemon juice

1 teaspoon raw honey

¼ preserved lemon, chopped (optional)

For the chicken:

2 tablespoons extra-virgin olive oil

6 boneless skinless chicken thighs

1 large red onion, peeled, trimmed, and sliced with Blade A

2 garlic cloves, minced

1 medium tomato, grated

⅓ cup low-sodium chicken stock (more as needed)

A pinch of saffron threads, mixed with 2 tablespoons water or 1 teaspoon ground turmeric

⅓ cup Kalamata olives, pitted

For the vegetable pasta:

3 taro roots, peeled, trimmed, and spiralized with Blade B

2 large carrots, peeled, trimmed, and spiralized with Blade B

1 small rutabaga, peeled, trimmed, and spiralized with Blade B

2 tablespoons cilantro, chopped, to garnish

Directions:

Place all chermoula ingredients in a blender or food processor and blend to a coarse paste; transfer to a bowl and set aside for 15–30 minutes for the flavors to blend.

Pat-dry the chicken thighs and place in a bowl. Add ½ cup chermoula and rub chicken to coat well; cover and refrigerate for 1–2 hours to marinate.

Heat olive oil in a Dutch oven or large heavy-based pot over a medium heat. Add chicken and sear, turning occasionally until lightly browned all over, about 6–7 minutes. Add onion and cook for 3–6 minutes, until translucent, then add garlic and tomato and cook, stirring for 1 minute. Pour in the chicken stock; add saffron and reduce heat to low. Cover with the lid and let simmer gently for 25–30 minutes. If necessary, add a little stock or water during cooking time, but make sure to keep the sauce thick.

Add olives and spiralized vegetables on top of the chicken, cover, and continue simmering until the vegetable pasta is tender, about 10 minutes.

Using pasta tongs, place pasta on serving plates; top with chicken and sauce; sprinkle with cilantro and serve immediately.

✔ Gluten-free ✔ Dairy-free
✔ Wheat-free   ✔ Low fat

Nutrition facts per serving (395 g):

calories 353 | total carbs 27g | protein 23g | total fat 17g | cholesterol 86mg | sodium 294mg

CHICKEN SOUVLAKI WITH LAHANOSALATA

Lahano means cabbage in Greek. Lahanosalata is Greek cabbage salad.

Serves 4
Prep Time: 15 minutes
Cook Time: 8 minutes

Ingredients:

For the skewers:

1 small lemon, quartered
3–4 garlic cloves
2–3 fresh bay leaves
2–3 sprigs fresh oregano or fresh thyme
1 teaspoon raw honey
1 teaspoon allspice berries
1 tablespoon sea salt
1 teaspoon black peppercorns
1½ pounds chicken breasts, cut into
    1½-inch pieces
¼ cup extra-virgin olive oil, for brushing
1 teaspoon dried oregano
3 tablespoons lemon juice
Wooden skewers, soaked in water for
    1–2 hours

For the salad:

2 large carrots, peeled, trimmed, and
    spiralized with Blade C

½ small white cabbage, shredded with
    Blade A
1 celery heart (the inner ribs), thinly sliced
1 medium fennel bulb, thinly sliced
1 green chili pepper, seeded and finely
    chopped
¼ cup fresh parsley, finely chopped

For the dressing:

⅓ cup plain Greek yogurt
½ teaspoon honey
½ teaspoon mustard
2 garlic cloves, minced
Juice and zest of 1 lemon
1 tablespoon extra-virgin olive oil
½ teaspoon paprika
Sea salt and freshly ground pepper, to taste
1 teaspoon celery or fennel seeds, crushed
    (optional)

Directions:

In a large saucepan combine 2 cups water with lemon, garlic, bay leaves, oregano, honey, allspice berries, salt, and peppercorns. Bring to a boil, turn off the heat, and let cool down to a room temperature. In a large glass container or resealable plastic bag, combine chicken and the cooled brine; refrigerate for 1–2 hours.

Cut carrots to bite-size pieces, place in a large bowl, and combine with the remaining salad ingredients.

Add all dressing ingredients to a food processor and blitz until smooth; drizzle over the salad and toss to coat. Season to taste, cover with plastic wrap and refrigerate until ready to serve.

In a small bowl, whisk together olive oil, oregano, and lemon juice with a fork.

Remove chicken with a slotted spoon and discard the brine. Pat chicken dry with kitchen paper towels and thread onto skewers; brush lightly with the olive oil mixture.

Spray a grill pan with cooking spray and heat over medium-high heat. Cook chicken skewers in batches, rotating often and basting with the olive oil and oregano mixture, until thoroughly cooked and nicely browned all over (about 8 minutes). For chicken, always make sure an instant-read thermometer reaches 165°.

Serve immediately with the salad.

✔ Gluten-free ✔ Wheat-free
✔ Low fat ✔ Low carb
✔ High protein

Nutrition facts per serving (395 g):

calories 346 | total carbs 15g | protein 42g | total fat 13g | cholesterol 99mg | sodium 198mg

ROSEMARY-LEMON CHICKEN WITH CARROT AND SWEET POTATO ROTINI

Serves 4
Prep Time: 20 minutes
Cook Time: 35–45 minutes

Ingredients:

For the marinade:

Juice and zest from 1 large lemon
3 tablespoons extra-virgin olive oil
2 fresh bay leaves
5 garlic cloves, peeled and roughly chopped
1½ tablespoons fresh rosemary leaves, chopped
Sea salt and freshly ground black pepper
⅓ cup white wine (optional)
1 small chili pepper, chopped (optional)

For the chicken:

4 (5–6 ounces each) boneless skinless
   chicken breasts
2 tablespoons olive oil
6–8 small shallots, peeled
½ celery heart (optional)
2 lemons, thinly sliced

Juice of 1 orange
1 teaspoon raw honey
¼–½ cup chicken broth, as needed
Sea salt and freshly ground black pepper

For the rotini:

1 tablespoon extra-virgin olive oil
1 shallot, finely chopped
1 garlic clove, minced
1 cup frozen peas
2 medium sweet potatoes, peeled, trimmed,
   spiralized with Blade B, and cut into
   1½-inch pieces
2 large carrots peeled, trimmed, spiralized
   with Blade B, and cut into 1½-inch pieces
Sea salt and freshly ground black pepper
1 sprig fresh rosemary, to garnish

Directions:

Place chicken breasts in a large lidded glass container or a bowl.

In a food processor or blender, combine all marinade ingredients and blitz until smooth; pour over the chicken breasts and stir to coat well. Cover and refrigerate for 1–2 hours; remove chicken and discard the marinade.

Heat 1 tablespoon olive oil in a large oven-proof skillet over a medium; add chicken breasts and sear until browned on both sides, 6–7 minutes. Transfer to a plate and set aside. Add remaining 1 tablespoon olive oil to the skillet and add shallots, celery heart, and lemons and cook, stirring often, until shallots and lemons begin to slightly caramelize, 6–7 minutes. Deglaze with orange juice; return chicken to the skillet, drizzle with honey, and add ¼ cup chicken broth. Season to taste, lower the heat, cover with the lid, and let simmer for about 20 minutes, until the chicken is fully cooked. Add a little chicken broth during cooking time if needed. Alternatively, place the skillet in a preheated oven and bake at 400°F for 20–25 minutes.

Meanwhile, prepare the carrot and sweet potato spirals. In a large skillet, heat olive oil over a medium heat; add shallot and garlic and cook for 2–3 minutes, until softened. Add frozen peas and vegetable pasta, season to taste and cook, tossing often, and adding a splash of water, if needed, for about 5–6 minutes or until the vegetables are just tender.

Serve chicken breasts with the vegetables, garnished with fresh rosemary.

✔ Gluten-free   ✔ Wheat-free   ✔ Low fat   ✔ High protein   ✔ Paleo

Nutrition facts per serving (360 g):

calories 381 | total carbs 31g | protein 37g | total fat 12g | cholesterol 81mg | sodium 200mg

CAJUN CHICKEN TENDERLOINS WITH BLACK RADISH, KOHLRABI, AND APPLE SLAW

Serves 4
Prep Time: 15 minutes
Cooking Time: 30–35 minutes

Ingredients:

For the chicken:
1½ pounds chicken tenderloins or boneless, skinless chicken breasts, sliced into strips
2–3 teaspoons Cajun seasoning
2 tablespoons olive oil
1 medium red bell pepper, diced
1 bunch scallions, trimmed and thinly sliced
1 jalapeño, seeded and finely chopped
2 garlic cloves, crushed
¼ cup white wine or low-sodium chicken stock
Sea salt and freshly ground black pepper

For the slaw:
1 kohlrabi bulb, peeled and spiralized with Blade C

1 Pink Lady apple, peeled, cored, and spiralized with Blade C
2 black radishes, peeled, trimmed, and spiralized with Blade C
¼ cup fresh parsley or cilantro, finely chopped
Sea salt and freshly ground black pepper

For the dressing:
3 tablespoons tangerine juice
2 tablespoons apple cider vinegar
1 teaspoon Dijon mustard
1 teaspoon honey
2 tablespoons olive oil
2 tablespoons lemon juice
1 garlic clove, minced

Directions:

Pat chicken dry and rub with Cajun seasoning.

Heat olive oil in a large heavy-bottom skillet over a medium-high heat; add chicken tenders and cook, turning often, until golden, 7–8 minutes. Add red pepper, scallions, and jalapeño and sauté until softened. Add garlic and cook for 1–2 minutes further. Pour in white wine or chicken stock, reduce heat to low and cover with a lid. Simmer gently for about 20–25 minutes, or until chicken is cooked through and most of the liquid has evaporated.

In the meantime, toss together all salad ingredients in a large bowl and season lightly. Place dressing ingredients in a blender and blitz until emulsified; drizzle over the salad and toss well.

Serve chicken with the salad.

✔ Gluten-free ✔ Wheat-free
✔ Low fat   ✔ High protein
✔ Paleo   ✔ Low carb

Nutrition facts per serving (405 g):

calories 382 | total carbs 18g
| protein 41g | total fat 16g |
cholesterol 97mg | sodium 163mg

CHICKEN SHEPHERD'S PIE WITH CAULIFLOWER, YAM, AND PARSNIP

Serves 6
Prep Time: 25 minutes
Cook Time: 1 hour 10 minutes

Ingredients:

For the filling:
2 tablespoons extra-virgin olive oil
3 leeks, white parts only, thinly sliced
1½ pounds ground chicken
6 ounces cremini mushrooms, sliced
2 garlic cloves, minced
2 tablespoons tomato paste
1 medium yellow squash, trimmed, spiralized with Blade C
Sea salt and freshly ground black pepper, to taste
1 cup low-sodium chicken stock
1 bay leaf
2 teaspoons each fresh thyme and flat-leaf parsley, finely chopped

2 teaspoons Worcestershire sauce
¼ cup mascarpone cheese (optional)

For the topping:
1 tablespoon grass-fed butter
1 shallot, finely chopped
2 cups cauliflower florets
1 medium yam, peeled, trimmed, and spiralized with Blade C
1 medium parsnip, peeled, trimmed, and spiralized with Blade C
Sea salt and freshly ground white pepper, to taste
2–3 tablespoons mascarpone cheese

✔ Dairy-free   ✔ Wheat-free   ✔ High protein   ✔ Paleo

Directions:

Preheat the oven to 375°F.

Heat olive oil in a large sauté pan over medium-high heat. Add the leeks and ground chicken and cook, stirring occasionally, until chicken has browned, about 7–8 minutes. Add mushrooms and garlic and continue cooking until the mushrooms are tender and moisture has evaporated.

Stir in the tomato paste and cook, stirring for 1 minute; add spiralized yellow squash, season to taste, and pour in the chicken stock. Add bay leaf, thyme, parsley, and Worcestershire; reduce heat, cover with a lid, and simmer for about 25 minutes, or until the sauce has thickened and the yellow squash has broken down completely.

Meanwhile, add cauliflower florets to a food processor or blender and process until it resembles rice. Add the spiralized yam and parsnip and pulse until vegetables are thoroughly blended together.

Melt butter in a large skillet over a medium heat and add the riced vegetables; cook, tossing often and adding a little water if too dry, until vegetables are soft, 7–8 minutes. Stir in mascarpone cheese and season to taste.

Transfer the filling to a baking dish; spoon the vegetable mixture on top and spread evenly. Bake until the filling is bubbling and the top is golden brown, about 20–25 minutes.

Nutrition facts per serving (395 g):

calories 426 | total carbs 34g | protein 25g | total fat 22g | cholesterol 119mg | sodium 138mg

CHICKEN PASTITSIO WITH CARROT AND POTATO

Pastitsio is a Greek baked pasta dish with ground meat and béchamel sauce. Here we substitute the pasta with spiralized carrots and potatoes.

Serves 8
Prep Time: 20 minutes
Cooking Time: 1 hour and 15 minutes

Ingredients:

For the filling:

2 tablespoons extra-virgin olive oil
1 pound boneless, skinless chicken breast, cut into small cubes
1 medium onion, finely chopped
1 large red bell pepper, chopped finely
2 slices uncured turkey bacon, diced
2 garlic cloves, minced
1 tomato, peeled and diced
1 tablespoon fresh oregano, finely chopped
2 tablespoons fresh flat-leaf parsley, finely chopped
Sea salt and freshly ground black pepper, to taste
½ cup chicken broth

For the vegetables:

3 large carrots, trimmed, peeled, and spiralized with Blade C
2 medium russet potatoes, peeled, trimmed, and spiralized with Blade C

For the béchamel sauce:

2 tablespoons butter
⅓ cup all-purpose flour
3 cups milk
2 cups low-sodium chicken broth
2 eggs, lightly beaten
1 cup Gruyère or Comté cheese, shredded
Sea salt and freshly ground white pepper, to taste
Baby arugula, to garnish

Directions:

Heat 1 tablespoon olive oil in a sauté pan over medium heat; add chicken and cook, stirring often, until lightly browned, 7–8 minutes; remove with a slotted spoon to a plate and set aside.

Heat the remaining 1 tablespoon oil in the same pan and add onion, bell pepper, and turkey bacon; sauté for about 3 minutes, stir in garlic and tomato and continue cooking for about 3–4 minutes. Return chicken to the pan, add oregano and parsley, season to taste, and pour in the chicken stock.Reduce heat to low, cover the pan with the lid, and let simmer until the chicken is cooked and the sauce has thickened, about 20 minutes.

Meanwhile, prepare the béchamel sauce. Melt the butter in a large sauce pan over medium-low heat; add flour and cook, stirring with a whisk, for 1–2 minutes, until a roux is formed. Pour in the milk and broth, and bring the sauce to a boil, stirring continuously until the cream thickens.

Remove saucepan from the heat and add the beaten eggs in a slow stream, stirring vigorously; stir in nutmeg and half of the cheese and set aside.

Preheat oven to 375°F.

In a large saucepan, bring 2 pints water to a boil over a medium heat. Add spiralized carrots and cook until just tender, 4–5 minutes; drain and place in a bowl. Repeat the process with the spiralized potatoes and place in another bowl; set aside.

Lightly grease a 3-quart baking dish and spread a few tablespoons of the béchamel sauce. Layer the potatoes, top with half of the chicken mixture, and spoon half of the béchamel sauce over it; sprinkle with a little cheese. Add a layer of carrots, then the remaining chicken mixture, and finish with béchamel. Sprinkle with the remaining cheese and bake for 20–25 minutes, or until the filling is bubbling and the top is golden brown. Remove from oven and let pastitsio sit for about 10 minutes before cutting into squares and serving with arugula.

✔ Gluten-free   ✔ Wheat-free
✔ Low fat   ✔ High protein

Nutrition facts per serving (380 g):

calories 343 | total carbs 25g | protein 25g | total fat 16g | cholesterol 120mg | sodium 220mg

MEAT

Herb-rolled Pork Tenderloin with Butternut Squash, Apples, and Beets ... 132

Paella con Costra (Paella with Crust) ... 134

Citrus and Garlic Roasted Lamb with Parsnip Rice ... 136

Lamb Souvlaki with Rutabaga Rice and Roasted Garlic and Mint Pesto ... 138

Spanish-style Dark Chocolate Beef Stew with Root Vegetables ... 140

Beef Sukiyaki ... 142

Kefta Tagine with Quince and Parsnip Couscous ... 144

Caribbean Meat and Sweet Potato Pies with Fruit Salsa ... 146

Malaysian Spicy Beef with Yellow Rice ... 148

Roasted Beef with Pineapple and Rutabaga Carrot Rice ... 150

HERB-ROLLED PORK TENDERLOIN WITH BUTTERNUT SQUASH, APPLES, AND BEETS

Serves 4
Prep Time:20 minutes
Cooking Time: 1 hour

Ingredients:

For the tenderloin:

1½ tablespoons wholegrain mustard

1 teaspoon raw honey

1 pork tenderloin (about 1¼–1½ pounds), trimmed

Sea salt and black pepper, to taste

¼ cup raw cashews

2 garlic cloves, minced

½ cup mixed fresh herbs (such as chives, parsley, oregano, thyme, or rosemary), finely chopped

1 tablespoon olive oil

2 tablespoons apple cider vinegar

½ cup white wine or chicken stock

For the vegetables:

1½ tablespoon extra-virgin olive oil

1 red onion, peeled, trimmed, and sliced with Blade A

2 large red beets, peeled, trimmed, and spiralized with Blade C

1 (5-inch) butternut squash neck, peeled, trimmed, and spiralized with blade C

Juice and zest of 1 orange

1 apple, cored and sliced with Blade A

2 tablespoons balsamic vinegar

Sea salt and black pepper, to taste

Directions:

Preheat the oven to 400°F.

In a small bowl, mix mustard and honey and set aside.

Lay the tenderloin on a large cutting board and trim excess fat; cut a lengthwise slit through the center, without going all the way through. Spread the meat flat, cover with plastic wrap, then flatten with a meat mallet or a rolling pin to a rectangle, about ¼-inch thick. Season with salt and pepper and spread the mustard mixture over the meat.

In a small bowl, combine the cashews, garlic, and fresh herbs, and spoon over the meat. Starting with the long side, roll up and tie with a kitchen twine or unwaxed dental floss at about 1–1½-inch intervals.

Heat olive oil in a large oven-safe skillet and quickly sear the meat roll. Add apple cider vinegar and wine or chicken stock and transfer to the oven. Roast for 45–50 minutes, or until the meat is tender and the thermometer reads 160°F.

Alternatively, skip the searing and place the meat roll on a greased shallow baking dish, pour in the wine or chicken stock, and roast as above.

Transfer meat to a platter; remove the twine and tent with aluminum foil. Let rest for about 10 minutes, while you prepare the vegetables.

Heat the olive oil in a large skillet over a medium-high heat and add sliced onion and sauté until softened and beginning to caramelize. Add spiralized beets, butternut squash, and orange zest and cook, tossing often for about 4–5 minutes. If the mixture becomes too dry, add a little orange juice at a time as needed. Stir in apples and balsamic vinegar and cook for about 2–3 minutes longer, until the apples and vegetables are just tender.

Cut the tenderloin into 1-inch slices, spoon over any pan juices, and serve with the vegetables.

✔ Gluten-free ✔ Dairy-free
✔ Wheat-free ✔ Paleo

Nutrition facts per serving (400 g):

calories 400 | total carbs 27g
| protein 32g | total fat 16g |
cholesterol 91mg | sodium 112mg

PAELLA CON COSTRA (PAELLA WITH CRUST)

Serves 6
Prep Time: 15 minutes
Cook Time: 30–35 minutes

Ingredients:

1 tablespoon extra-virgin olive oil
4 ounces botifarra (Spanish white sausage)
  or chorizo
½ pound lean pork, cut into ½-inch cubes
½ pound skinless boneless chicken breast, cut
  into ½-inch cubes
3 garlic cloves, minced
2 large tomatoes, cut in half and grated
½ cup green beans, cut into 1-inch pieces
½ cup frozen baby lima beans
Juice and zest of 1 lemon
Generous pinch saffron threads
Sea salt and freshly ground black pepper,
  to taste
1½ cups low sodium chicken stock
  (more as needed)
2 large turnips, peeled, trimmed and
  spiralized with Blade C
¼ cup fresh parsley, chopped
5 large eggs, lightly beaten with 2
  tablespoons water

Directions:

Heat olive oil in a large oven-safe skillet over medium-high heat and add sausage, pork, and chicken pieces and cook, tossing, until lightly browned, 3–4 minutes. Add garlic and tomato pulp and cook, stirring occasionally for about 5 minutes, until slightly reduced. Add green beans, baby lima beans, lemon juice and zest, and saffron threads; season to taste and pour in the chicken stock and cover with a lid.

Reduce the heat to medium-low and simmer until the meat is cooked through, about 12–15 minutes. Stir in the turnip rice and parsley and a little stock or water if the mixture is too dry and turn off the heat.

Meanwhile, preheat the oven to 375°F.

Season the beaten eggs to taste and pour over the meat and rice mixture. Place the skillet, uncovered, in the oven and bake for 8–10 minutes, until the egg crust is set and nicely browned.

Serve immediately.

✔ Gluten-free ✔ Dairy-free ✔ Wheat-free ✔ Low carb ✔ High protein

Nutrition facts per serving (350 g):

calories 306 | total carbs 12g | protein 29g | total fat 16g | cholesterol 239mg | sodium 402mg

CITRUS AND GARLIC ROASTED LAMB WITH PARSNIP RICE

Serves 8
Prep Time: 15 minutes
Cooking Time: 30–40 minutes

Ingredients:

For the lamb:

Zest and juice of 2 lemons
Zest and juice of 1 orange
Zest and juice of 1 lime
2 teaspoons dried oregano or dried thyme
1 tablespoon extra-virgin olive oil
1 (5½–6 pounds) bone-in whole leg of
   lamb, trimmed of excess fat
8 garlic cloves, sliced into thirds lengthwise
Sea salt and freshly ground black pepper, to
   taste

For the rice:

4 parsnips, peeled, trimmed, and spiralized
   with Blade B
1 tablespoons extra-virgin olive oil
2 shallots, peeled and chopped
1 jalapeño pepper, seeded and diced small
1 medium red bell pepper, seeded and diced
   small
1 medium green bell pepper, seeded and
   diced small
Sea salt and freshly ground black pepper, to
   taste

✔ Gluten-free ✔ Dairy-free
✔ Wheat-free ✔ Low fat
✔ High protein ✔ Low carb

Directions:

Preheat oven to 350°F and lightly grease a roasting pan that will fit the leg of lamb.

In a small bowl, combine the citrus juices and set aside. In another small bowl, combine oregano, citrus zests, and olive oil.

With a sharp small knife, cut slits in the lamb, spacing them a few inches apart, and push in garlic slivers; season with salt and pepper and rub meat with the citrus mixture. Transfer to the prepared pan and pour ½ cup water into the pan. Place in the oven and roast until the meat is done to your liking, approximately 15–20 minutes for medium rare; 20–25 minutes for medium, and 25–30 minutes for well done. During the cooking process, pour a few tablespoons of the citrus juice over the lamb every 5–10 minutes. Allow lamb to rest about 10 minutes before carving.

For the parsnip rice, place spiralized parsnips in a food processor and pulse until they resemble large rice grains.

Heat olive oil in a large skillet and add shallot and diced peppers; cook for 2–3 minutes until softened. Add parsnip rice, season, and cook, adding a little water if too dry, until tender.

Serve lamb with the parsnip rice.

Nutrition facts per serving (325 g):

calories 390 | total carbs 13g | protein 47g | total fat 15g | cholesterol 145mg | sodium 191mg

Nutrition facts per serving for the sauce (20 g):

calories 15 | total carbs 1g | protein 0g | total fat 1g | cholesterol 3mg | sodium 69mg

LAMB SOUVLAKI WITH RUTABAGA RICE AND ROASTED GARLIC AND MINT PESTO

Serves 4
Prep Time: 20 minutes
Cooking Time: 15–17 minutes

Ingredients:

For the lamb:

1½–2 pounds boneless lamb, trimmed and cut into 1½-inch cubes

2–3 sprigs each fresh oregano and fresh thyme

2–3 tablespoons extra virgin olive oil

3 large garlic cloves, minced

1 teaspoon honey

Zest and juice of 1 lemon

1 large red onion, cut into 1–1½-inch dice

Sea salt and freshly ground black pepper

For the roasted garlic pesto:

1 garlic bulb

⅓ cup extra virgin olive oil

3 tablespoons shelled pistachios

3 tablespoons cashews

⅔ packed cup fresh mint leaves

⅓ cup fresh parsley

Juice and zest of 1 lemon

Sea salt and freshly ground black pepper

For the rice:

2 small rutabagas, trimmed, peeled, and spiralized with Blade C

1 red onion, peeled, trimmed, and sliced with Blade A

⅓ cup pitted Kalamata olives, chopped

1 medium cucumber, diced

1 tomato, diced

1–2 handfuls arugula

Plain Greek yogurt, to serve (optional)

✔ Gluten-free   ✔ Dairy-free   ✔ Paleo   ✔ Wheat-free
✔ Low fat   ✔ High protein   ✔ Low carb

Directions:

Place lamb, oregano, and thyme sprigs in a large Ziploc bag. In a small bowl, whisk together olive oil, garlic, honey, and lemon zest and juice and pour over the lamb. Mix together and refrigerate for at least 1 hour.

For the pesto, preheat oven to 425°F. Slice off the top of the garlic bulb, brush generously with olive oil and wrap in a piece of aluminum foil. Place on a baking sheet and bake for about 25–30 minutes, until tender; let cool for a few minutes before gently squeezing the cloves out. Add roasted garlic to a blender or food processor together with the rest of the pesto ingredients. Pulse until well combined, season with salt and pepper, and adjust the consistency to your liking by adding a little water. Transfer to a bowl and set aside.

Add spiralized rutabagas to a food processor and pulse until they resemble rice grains.

Bring 4 cups water to a boil in a large saucepan over a medium-high heat; add a dash of salt and the rutabaga rice. Boil for 4–5 minutes, until just tender, drain, and place in a large salad bowl. Set aside to cool to a room temperature.

Thread the marinated lamb cubes onto metal skewers, alternating with onion pieces; season to taste and cook in pre-heated griddle pan for about 12 minutes, turning often, until cooked to the desired doneness.

Add the sliced onion, Kalamata olives, cucumber, tomato, and arugula to the cooled rutabaga rice, drizzle with a little pesto and toss gently.

Serve lamb skewers immediately over the rutabaga rice salad with the pesto on the side and a dollop of plain Greek yogurt, if desired. Refrigerate any remaining pesto for up to 5 days.

Nutrition facts per serving
(395 g):

calories 323 | total carbs 14g
| protein 37g | total fat 12g |
cholesterol 107mg |
sodium 303mg

Nutrition facts per serving for
the pesto sauce (10 g):

calories 46 | total carbs 1g
| protein 1g | total fat 5g |
cholesterol 0mg |
sodium 1mg

SPANISH-STYLE DARK CHOCOLATE BEEF STEW WITH ROOT VEGETABLES

Serves 6
Prep Time: 10 minutes
Cooking Time: 30–35 minutes

Ingredients:

For the beef:

2 tablespoons raw cacao powder

¼ teaspoon cayenne pepper

1½ pounds beef tenderloin, trimmed and cut into 1½-inch cubes

1 tablespoon extra-virgin olive oil

1 leek, white part only, sliced thin

3 garlic cloves, unpeeled

Juice and zest of 1 blood orange

3–4 cups low sodium beef broth (or dark beer), as needed

1 bay leaf

A pinch of nutmeg

2½-ounces dark chocolate (70% cocoa solids), broken into squares

Sea salt and freshly ground black pepper, to taste

For the root vegetables:

1 tablespoon extra-virgin olive oil

1 small red onion, peeled, trimmed, and sliced with Blade A

2 celery roots, peeled, trimmed, and spiralized with Blade C

2 large carrots, peeled, trimmed, and spiralized with Blade C

1 small yucca (or 1 small sweet potato), peeled, trimmed, and spiralized with Blade C

1 small sprig fresh thyme

3 tablespoons fresh parsley, chopped, to serve

Directions:

In a small bowl, combine cacao powder with cayenne pepper and rub the beef cubes all over with the mixture.

Heat olive oil in a large sauté pan or Dutch oven over medium-high heat; add the beef and cook, stirring occasionally, for about 8–10 minutes. Transfer to a plate with a slotted spoon, leaving any juices in the pan.

Thread unpeeled garlic cloves onto a wooden toothpick and add to the same pan, together with the leeks; sauté until softened, 3–4 minutes. Deglaze with the blood orange juice and return beef to the pan. Pour in enough beef broth to just cover the meat, and add bay leaf, nutmeg, chocolate, and orange zest. Season to taste, cover with a lid, and reduce the heat to low and let simmer until the beef is very tender, 20–25 minutes. Check the stew during cooking time and add more broth as necessary. Remove and discard garlic cloves and bay leaf.

For the root vegetables, heat oil in a large skillet and sauté the red onion until it begins to caramelize. Add the spiralized root vegetables, thyme, and a splash of beef broth or water and cook, tossing often, until vegetables are just tender.

Serve beef stew over the vegetables, sprinkled with fresh parsley.

✔ Gluten-free ✔ Dairy-free
✔ Wheat-free ✔ Low fat

Nutrition facts per serving (400 g):

calories 406 | total carbs 30g
| protein 31g | total fat 19g |
cholesterol 76mg | sodium 381mg

BEEF SUKIYAKI

There are two main types of tofu, which differ in texture. The English names vary, but in Japanese they are called momen and kinu. Momen tofu, also called "regular," "coarse," "spongy," "cotton," or "wool" tofu, is drained and pressed as the tofu is forming so the excess liquid runs out.

Serves 4
Prep Time: 20 minutes
Cook Time: 10 minutes

Ingredients:

½ packet (6 ounces) firm tofu (preferably momen), cut into thin slices

1½ tablespoons neutral cooking oil

1 tablespoon shoyu sauce (or tamari for wheat-free diet)

1 pound marbled beef, such as rib eye, trimmed and thinly sliced

1 bunch scallions, sliced at an angle into 1-inch pieces

½ cup canned bamboo shoots, drained and sliced

1 cup shiitake mushrooms, stemmed and caps cut in half

4 baby bok choy, sliced

1 small package Shimeji or Enoki mushrooms, trimmed

1 medium Korean radish (or 1 Opo squash), trimmed, peeled, and spiralized with Blade D

2 large carrots, peeled, trimmed, and spiralized with Blade D

For the sauce:

1¼ cups water

½ heaped teaspoon instant dashi powder (MSG-free)*

¼ cup mirin

1 tablespoon brown sugar

2 tablespoons shoyu sauce (or tamari for wheat-free diet), optional

*If dashi is not available, use 1 cup beef broth mixed with 1 tablespoon shoyu sauce.

Directions:

Line a rimmed baking sheet with 2–3 layers kitchen paper towels. Cut tofu into ½–¾-inch slices and place on the paper. Cover with another double layer of paper towels, place a baking sheet on top of the tofu, and weigh down with dishes or food cans. Let stand for 15–20 minutes, until the excess water has drained; pat dry with kitchen paper towels and cut into cubes.

In a small saucepan, mix water and dashi powder, add mirin, brown sugar, and shoyu sauce. Bring to a boil over a medium-high heat and stir to dissolve sugar; remove from heat and set aside.

Heat the oil in a lidded large heavy-bottom skillet (preferably cast-iron), over medium-high heat. Add the sliced beef and sear, adding a little of the sauce, until lightly browned, about 1 minute per side; transfer to a platter and keep warm.

Add scallions to the skillet and cook for 1 minute, until softened; add tofu, bamboo shoots, shiitake mushrooms, and bok choy and cook for 2–3 minutes, stirring occasionally, until the tofu is lightly browned and vegetables begin to wilt. Return beef to the skillet, add shimeji mushrooms, radish, and carrot noodles, pour in the remaining sauce, and cover with the lid. Reduce heat to low and let simmer for 2–3 minutes, until the noodles are just tender.

Serve immediately.

✔ Gluten-free   ✔ Dairy-free
✔ Wheat-free   ✔ Low fat
✔ High protein

Nutrition facts per serving (410 g):

calories 375 | total carbs 30g
| protein 33g | total fat 15g |
cholesterol 76mg | sodium 667mg

KEFTA TAGINE WITH QUINCE AND PARSNIP COUSCOUS

This dish is like Moroccan meatballs cooked in a tagine pot.

Serves 4
Prep Time: 20 minutes
Cooking Time: 25–30 minutes

Ingredients:

For the meatballs:

3 tablespoons extra-virgin olive oil, divided
1 shallot, peeled and finely chopped
1 (1½-inch) piece fresh ginger, minced
2 garlic cloves, minced
1 small sweet potato, peeled, trimmed, and
    spiralized with Blade C
2 tablespoons each cilantro, fresh mint, and
    fresh parsley, chopped
1 pound lean ground beef
Sea salt and freshly ground black pepper,
    to taste
1 large onion, peeled and sliced with Blade A
1 teaspoon ground turmeric
½ teaspoon ground cinnamon

1 teaspoon ground cumin
1 teaspoon ground coriander
½ teaspoon ground caraway seeds
⅓ cup tomato sauce
1 teaspoon harissa paste (more to taste)
2 quinces, peeled, cored, and quartered (if
    not available, use Bartlett pears or apples)
1 teaspoon honey

For the couscous:

3 large parsnips, peeled, trimmed, and
    spiralized with Blade C
1 tablespoon ghee or extra-virgin olive oil
Juice of 1 lemon
1 teaspoon orange blossom water (optional)
Cilantro, to garnish

Directions:

Heat 1 tablespoon olive oil in a medium skillet over medium-high heat and add shallot, ginger, and garlic; sauté until softened, 2–3 minutes. Add sweet potato spirals and a little water and cook, stirring often until tender, 4–5 minutes. Remove from heat, let cool for a few minutes, and transfer to a food processor; add parsley, cilantro, and mint, and blend together to combine.

Transfer sweet potato mixture to a large bowl; add ground beef, season to taste, and mix well with your hands; form into 1½-inch balls, flatten slightly, and set aside.

Heat the remaining 2 tablespoons oil in a tagine pot or Dutch oven over a medium-low heat. Add sliced onions and sauté until translucent; add meatballs and cook, turning around occasionally, until lightly browned. Stir in the turmeric, cinnamon, cumin, coriander, and caraway seeds and cook for 1 minute until fragrant. Add tomato sauce, harissa, and quinces; drizzle with honey and enough water to just cover the meatballs. Cover the tagine with the lid and reduce the heat to low; let simmer for about 20 minutes.

In the meantime, pulse spiralized parsnips in a blender or food processor until they resemble couscous grains. Heat ghee in a large skillet, add the couscous and 2–3 tablespoons lemon juice, and cook for about 5 minutes, until tender. Stir in orange blossom water, if using, and toss.

Serve meatballs over the couscous, garnished with fresh cilantro.

✔ Gluten-free ✔ Dairy-free ✔ Paleo ✔ Wheat-free ✔ Low fat

Nutrition facts per serving (370 g):

calories 427 | total carbs 38g | protein 27g | total fat 20g | cholesterol 69mg | sodium 110mg

CARIBBEAN MEAT AND SWEET POTATO PIES WITH FRUIT SALSA

Serves 4
Prep Time: 15 minutes
Cooking Time: 25–39 minutes

Ingredients:

For the salsa:

1 chayote or cucumber, diced
1 mango, peeled and diced
1 green chili, seeded and finely chopped
1 cup pineapple, diced
3 scallions, thinly sliced
2 tablespoons fresh mint or cilantro, finely
    chopped
Juice and zest of 1 lime
Sea salt and freshly ground white pepper, to
    taste

For the filling:

1½ tablespoons rapeseed or canola oil
1 medium onion, peeled and finely chopped
1 small carrot, peeled and finely diced
1 scotch bonnet pepper, seeded and finely
    chopped (optional)
1 (2-inch) piece fresh ginger, minced
1 pound lean ground beef or lamb
2 garlic cloves, minced
2 teaspoons Caribbean jerk seasoning
Sea salt and freshly ground black pepper,
    to taste

For the cakes:

1 tablespoon rapeseed or canola oil
1 garlic clove, minced
1 green chili, seeded and finely chopped
4 medium sweet potatoes, peeled, trimmed,
    and spiralized with Blade C
1 egg, lightly beaten
2 tablespoons finely chopped cilantro
Sea salt and freshly ground black pepper,
    to taste

✔ Gluten-free ✔ Dairy-free
✔ Paleo ✔ Wheat-free
✔ Low fat

Directions:

In a bowl, combine all salsa ingredients; season to taste and set aside (may be prepared 2–3 hours in advance and refrigerated until needed).

For the filling, heat oil in a large heavy-bottom skillet over medium-high heat and add garlic, onion, and carrot. Sauté until softened, then add pepper and ginger and cook for 1–2 minutes; add ground beef or lamb and season to taste. Cook, stirring often to break any lumps, about 5–7 minutes, until the meat begins to brown. Stir in Caribbean jerk seasoning, and cook for further 1–2 minutes. Set aside.

Preheat oven to 375°F; lightly grease a standard muffin pan and set aside.

For the cakes, heat oil in a large skillet and add garlic, chili, and spiralized potatoes. Cook, tossing often, for about 5–7 minutes, or until the potato is tender. Add a little water to the pan if necessary. Transfer to a bowl and let cool for 5–10 minutes; add the beaten egg, season to taste, and mix well with a potato masher.

Add enough sweet potato mixture to the muffin cups to fill halfway, pressing down with a spoon. Add 2 tablespoons of the filling on top and add more of the sweet potatoes to enclose the filling completely.

Place pan in the oven and bake for about 10–12 minutes, or until golden brown. Transfer to a wire rack and let cool for 5 minutes before removing the cakes onto plates.

Garnish cakes with cilantro and serve with salsa on the side.

Nutrition facts per serving for the cakes (310 g):

calories 376 | total carbs 31g | protein 28g | total fat 15g | cholesterol 122mg | sodium 173mg

Nutrition facts per serving for the salsa (71 g): 8 servings

calories 30 | total carbs 8g | protein 1g | total fat 0g | cholesterol 0mg | sodium 2mg

MALAYSIAN SPICY BEEF WITH YELLOW RICE

Serves 4
Prep Time: 15 minutes
Cooking Time: 15 minutes

Ingredients:

For the beef:

1½ tablespoons coconut oil

1 large red onion, peeled and sliced with
  Blade A

1 (2-inch) piece fresh ginger, minced

2 lemongrass stalks, tough outer leaves
  removed and finely chopped

2–3 garlic cloves, minced

1 pound lean beef, cut into about 3 inch
  long, ½-inch thick strips

1 teaspoon ground coriander

1 tablespoon tamarind paste, mixed with ½
  cup water

1 tablespoon sugar

1½ teaspoon lime zest

1 bay leaf

1 cup coconut milk

Sea salt and freshly ground black pepper,
  to taste

For the rice:

1 teaspoon turmeric

½ teaspoon ground cinnamon

¼ teaspoon ground cardamom

1 pinch saffron strands, mixed with
  3 tablespoons water (optional)

Pinch ground cloves

1 tablespoon coconut oil

2 shallots, finely chopped

2 garlic cloves, thinly sliced

3 medium turnips, peeled, trimmed, and
  spiralized with Blade B

2 tablespoons coconut cream

1 teaspoon rosewater (optional)

To serve: (optional)

Toasted coconut, to serve

Chopped cilantro, to garnish

Directions:

In a large lidded sauté pan or Dutch oven, heat coconut oil and add sliced onion. Cook until softened, 3–4 minutes; add ginger, lemongrass, and garlic, and cook 2–3 minutes, stirring often. Add beef and cook until browned, about 6–8 minutes. Stir in coriander, tamarind, sugar, lime zest, and bay leaf; cook for 2 minutes and add coconut milk and enough water to just cover the meat. Bring to a boil, reduce heat, cover, and simmer until the sauce has thickened and beef is tender, 15–20 minutes.

In the meantime, prepare the rice. In a small bowl, combine turmeric, cinnamon, cardamom, saffron, and cloves and mix to a paste.

Heat coconut oil in a large heavy-bottom skillet over a medium-high heat. Add shallots and garlic and cook for 1–2 minutes; stir in the spice paste and cook for 1 minute further, until fragrant. Add turnip rice and cook, tossing often and adding a splash of water if too dry for 3–4 minutes, until tender. Stir in the coconut cream and rosewater, if using, cook for 2 minutes, and turn off the heat.

Serve beef with the turnip rice, garnished with toasted coconut and chopped cilantro.

✔ Gluten-free   ✔ Dairy-free
✔ Paleo   ✔ Wheat-free

Nutrition facts per serving (365 g):

calories 387 | total carbs 21g
| protein 27g | total fat 22g |
cholesterol 76mg | sodium 147mg

ROASTED BEEF WITH PINEAPPLE AND RUTABAGA CARROT RICE

Serves 8
Prep Time: 15 minutes
Cooking Time: 15 minutes

Ingredients:

For the beef:

1 (about 2½-3 pounds) beef tenderloin, trimmed
3 sprigs fresh rosemary, finely chopped
Sea salt and crushed black pepper
2 tablespoons olive oil
⅓ cup pineapple juice
½ cup beef broth
¼ cup balsamic vinegar
1 teaspoon arrowroot powder potato starch, mixed with ¼ cup cold water

For the rice:

2 large carrot, spiralized with Blade C
2 rutabagas, spiralized with Blade C
1 tablespoon extra-virgin olive oil
1 red onion, sliced with Blade A
2 celery ribs, chopped finely
2 cups pineapple chunks
2 tablespoons raw honey
Sea salt and freshly ground black pepper, to taste
3 tablespoons fresh chives, finely chopped

Directions:

Preheat oven to 425°F; lightly grease a roasting pan and set aside.

Season beef tenderloin with salt and pepper and rub with the chopped rosemary.

Heat olive oil in a large skillet over medium-high heat; add meat and quickly sear until browned on all sides. Transfer to the prepared roasting pan. Pour in the pineapple juice and roast for 35–40 minutes for medium rare or 45–50 minutes for medium. Transfer to a cutting board and tent with aluminum foil; let stand for 10–15 minutes.

Meanwhile, prepare the rice. Place the spiralized carrots and rutabagas in a food processor or blender and pulse until they resemble rice-grains.

Heat olive oil in a large heavy-bottom skillet over a medium-high heat. Add onion and celery and sauté until softened. Add pineapple chunks, drizzle with honey, and cook until pineapple begins to caramelize. Add vegetable rice and season to taste. Cook, tossing occasionally, until just tender. Add a little pineapple juice if too dry. Remove from heat, stir in the chives, and set aside.

Pour the pan sauces into a small saucepan, add broth and balsamic vinegar, and bring to a simmer. Stir in arrowroot slurry and simmer, stirring, for about 1–2 minutes, until sauce thickens.

Slice the meat and serve with the sauce and pineapple rice.

✔ Gluten-free	✔ Dairy-free
✔ Paleo	✔ Wheat-free
✔ Low fat	✔ High protein

Nutrition facts per serving (365 g):

calories 360 | total carbs 23g | protein 34g | total fat 15g | cholesterol 95mg | sodium 152mg

VEGETARIAN MEALS AND SIDES

IMAM BAYILDI WITH ZUCCHINI AND YOGURT-TAHINI SAUCE

This is a traditional Turkish dish.

Serves 4
Prep Time: 15 minutes
Cooking Time: 45–50 minutes

Ingredients:

For the eggplants:

8 miniature round eggplants (or 4 long, slim ones), stem ends cut off
Juice of 1 lemon
1 teaspoon sea salt
4 large garlic cloves, peeled and quartered lengthwise
4 tablespoons olive oil, divided
1 medium red onion, peeled, trimmed, and spiralized with Blade A
1 red bell pepper, seeded and diced small
1 garlic clove, minced
1 green chili pepper, seeded and finely chopped
1 teaspoon paprika
1 teaspoon ground cumin
4 medium ripe tomatoes or 1 (15-ounce) can tomatoes, diced
1 teaspoon honey or sugar
1 bay leaf
2 sprigs fresh oregano

3 tablespoons fresh flat-leaf parsley, finely chopped

For the zucchini:

1 scallion, thinly sliced
2 medium zucchini, trimmed and spiralized with Blade C
1 tablespoon fresh basil leaves, thinly sliced
Sea salt and freshly ground black pepper, to taste

For the tahini sauce:

½ cup Greek yogurt
1 ½ tablespoons tahini
1 garlic clove, minced
1 teaspoon raw honey
⅛ teaspoon of each cayenne pepper and ground cumin
1 tablespoon olive oil
2–3 tablespoons lime juice
Sea salt and freshly ground black pepper, to taste

Directions:

Peel 3–4 alternate strips off the eggplants lengthwise and make 1-inch incisions in the middle of each strip. Place eggplants in a large bowl and pour in enough cold water to cover them. Add the lemon juice and 1 teaspoon salt; place a plate on top of the eggplants to keep them immersed and let soak for 15 minutes.

Drain and pat eggplants dry with kitchen paper towels then push a piece of garlic into each slit.

In a large oven-safe skillet, heat 2 tablespoons olive oil over a medium-high heat and add the eggplants; fry, turning regularly, for 7–8 minutes, until nicely browned all over. Transfer to a plate and set aside.

Add 1 tablespoon olive oil and the sliced onion to the same skillet and sauté over medium heat until softened. Add diced bell pepper, garlic, and chili, and continue cooking until softened. Stir in paprika and cumin and cook for about 30 seconds, until fragrant. Add tomatoes and honey, season to taste, and add bay leaf and oregano. Lower the heat, cover skillet with the lid and cook, stirring occasionally for 7–8 minutes. Return eggplants to the skillet, scatter chopped parsley on top and cook, covered, for about 25–30 minutes, or until the sauce is reduced and eggplants are cooked through. Alternatively, place skillet in a preheated 350°F oven and bake for 35–40 minutes.

Meanwhile, prepare the yogurt-tahini sauce. Place all sauce ingredients in a blender and pulse until smooth; adjust seasoning and set aside.

Heat the remaining 1 tablespoon olive oil in a large skillet over a medium-high heat; add scallion, zucchini, and basil and cook, tossing, for 4–5 minutes, until just tender.

Serve eggplants and zucchini with tahini sauce on the side.

✔ Gluten-free ✔ Low fat
✔ Wheat-free ✔ Low calorie

Nutrition facts per serving (420 g):

calories 214 | total carbs 22g | protein 4g | total fat 14g | cholesterol 0mg | sodium 22mg

Nutrition facts per serving for the sauce (15 g):

calories 24 | total carbs 1g | protein 1g | total fat 2g | cholesterol 1mg | sodium 6mg

TOMATO AND BLOOD ORANGE CELERY ROOT SPAGHETTI

Serves 4
Prep Time: 15 minutes
Cooking Time: 15–20 minutes

Ingredients:

2 tablespoons olive oil
1 shallot, finely chopped
1 small jalapeño pepper, seeded and finely
    chopped
2–3 garlic cloves, slivered
¼ cup sun-dried tomatoes in olive oil,
    drained and chopped
2 cups heirloom or grape tomatoes, halved
2 tablespoon of each fresh oregano, basil and
    flat leaf parsley, finely chopped
Juice of 2 blood oranges plus 1 teaspoon zest
1 teaspoon raw honey
Sea salt and freshly ground black pepper to
    taste
2 celery roots, peeled, trimmed, and
    spiralized with Blade C
2–3 tablespoons ground raw cashews, to
    serve
Fresh basil leaves, to garnish

Directions:

Heat olive oil in a large saucepan over a medium heat; add shallot, jalapeño, and garlic and sauté until softened. Stir in the sun-dried and heirloom tomatoes and cook, stirring occasionally, for 5–6 minutes, until softened.

Add the fresh herbs, orange juice, and honey; season to taste, lower the heat, cover with a lid, and simmer for 7–8 minutes, until reduced. Add celery root, toss, and simmer, covered, for 5–6 minutes longer or until the celery root spaghetti are just tender.

Sprinkle with ground cashews and serve garnished with basil leaves.

✔ Gluten-free ✔ Dairy-free ✔ Paleo ✔ Wheat-free ✔ Low fat ✔ Vegan

Nutrition facts per serving (300 g):

calories 214 | total carbs 28g | protein 5g | total fat 11g | cholesterol 0mg | sodium 180mg

SPICY VEGETABLE AND RED RICE BOWL WITH ALMOND BUTTER SAUCE

Serves 4
Prep Time: 10 minutes
Cook Time: none

Ingredients:

2 cups cooked red or wild rice
2 cups cooked quinoa or mixed super grains
   (quinoa, mullet, and buckwheat)
2 medium cucumbers, trimmed and
   spiralized with Blade C
1 Korean radish, peeled, trimmed, and
   spiralized with Blade D
2 large carrots, peeled, trimmed, and
   spiralized with Blade D
4 tablespoons blanched almonds, roughly
   chopped

For the sauce:
¼ cup almond milk
3 tablespoons almond butter
3 tablespoons lemon juice, freshly squeezed
½ cup orange juice, freshly squeezed
1 teaspoon hot sauce (or to taste)
1 garlic clove, crushed
1 teaspoon ginger, minced
Sea salt and freshly ground white pepper, to
   taste

For the garnish:
Kimchi, scallions, hard-boiled eggs, toasted
   slivered almonds

Directions:

Divide cooked rice, quinoa, cucumbers, radish, carrots, and almonds between 4 bowls.

In a blender, combine all sauce ingredients and blitz until smooth. Season to taste and if necessary, adjust thickness with a splash of water.

Serve bowls topped with the sauce and the desired garnishes.

✔ Gluten-free ✔ Dairy-free ✔ Wheat-free ✔ Low fat

Nutrition facts per serving (380 g):

calories 286 | total carbs 49g | protein 11g | total fat 7g | cholesterol 0mg | sodium 53mg

Nutrition facts per serving for the sauce (18 g):

calories 25 | total carbs 2g | protein 1g | total fat 2g | cholesterol 0mg | sodium 3mg

TARO ROOT, ZUCCHINI, AND EGGPLANT MOUSSAKA

Serves 8
Prep Time: 20 minutes
Cooking Time: 1 hour

Ingredients:

For the sauce:

3 tablespoons extra virgin olive oil
1 red onion, peeled, trimmed, and sliced with Blade A
1 large carrot, peeled and diced small
1 red bell pepper, seeded and diced small
2–3 garlic cloves, minced
3 cups button mushrooms, chopped
1 teaspoon paprika
½ teaspoon ground cinnamon
¼ teaspoon ground allspice
1 (15-ounce) can tomato sauce
1 tablespoon fresh oregano leaves, chopped
1 fresh bay leaf
¼ cup flat-leaf parsley, finely chopped
Sea salt and freshly ground black pepper
⅓ cup kefalotiri or other hard, sharp cheese, such a Pecorino, grated

For the vegetable layers:

3 long, thin eggplants, peeled, trimmed, and sliced with Blade A
Juice of 1 small lemon
1 taro root (3 cups sliced), peeled, trimmed, and sliced with Blade A
3 medium zucchini, trimmed and sliced with Blade A

For the topping:

2 cups plain Greek yogurt
1 teaspoon arrowroot powder
A pinch of baking powder
½ teaspoon paprika
A dash of cinnamon
3 large eggs, lightly beaten
Sea salt and freshly ground black pepper

Directions:

In a large heavy-bottom skillet, heat the olive oil over a medium-high heat; add sliced onion and sauté for 4–5 minutes, until soft. Add diced carrot and bell pepper and cook for 3–4 minutes, then add garlic and mushrooms and cook until mushrooms are tender, 5–6 minutes.

Stir in paprika, cinnamon, and allspice and cook for 1 minute, then pour in the tomato sauce. Season to taste, add oregano and bay leaf, reduce heat to low, and simmer for 8–10 minutes, until thickened. Stir in the parsley and adjust seasoning.

Preheat oven to 350°F. Lightly grease a 9 x 13-inch baking dish and set aside.

Add eggplant slices to a bowl, fill with enough water to cover them, and add lemon juice; soak for 10–15 minutes and drain. Transfer to a plate and set aside.

Meanwhile, in a large saucepan, bring 4 cups water to a boil and add sliced taro roots; cook for 2–3 minutes, until just tender; drain and set aside.

Bring 4 cups water to a boil in another large saucepan, add the eggplant, and cook for about 3 minutes, until tender; drain and set aside.

Place all topping ingredients in a food processor or blender and pulse until smooth; season to taste and set aside.

Spread a few tablespoons of the sauce into the prepared baking dish. Layer taro slices on top and spoon over ⅓ of the sauce. Sprinkle with 2 tablespoons cheese and place a layer of the eggplant slices. Spoon half of the remaining sauce on top, sprinkle with 2 tablespoons cheese, and arrange a layer of zucchini slices. Spread the remaining sauce, pour the topping over and sprinkle with remaining cheese.

Place Moussaka in the oven and bake for about 25–30 minutes, or until the zucchini are cooked and the top is golden brown.

Allow to rest for about 10 minutes before cutting into squares and serving.

✔ Gluten-free
✔ Wheat-free
✔ Low fat

Nutrition facts per serving (440 g):

calories 254 | total carbs 33g
| protein 11g | total fat 10g |
cholesterol 87mg | sodium 143mg

ISLAND SPAGHETTI WITH ROASTED HEIRLOOM TOMATOES, OLIVES, AND HERBS

Serves 4
Prep Time: 15 minutes
Cooking Time: 20 minutes

Ingredients:

3 cups heirloom cherry tomatoes, larger ones
    cut in half
A few sprigs of each fresh thyme and oregano
4 tablespoons extra-virgin olive oil, divided
Salt and freshly ground pepper, to taste
2 garlic cloves, slivered
Juice and zest of 1 lemon
1 fresh bay leaf
2 medium green zucchini, trimmed and
    spiralized with Blade C
2 medium yellow zucchini, trimmed and
    spiralized with Blade C
⅓ cup mixed pitted green and Kalamata
    olives, sliced
3 tablespoons pine nuts, lightly toasted
Fresh basil leaves, chopped, to garnish
⅔ cup mozzarella, string, or goat cheese,
    optional

Directions:

Preheat oven to 400°F.

In a rimmed baking sheet, combine tomatoes, thyme, and oregano; drizzle with 3 tablespoons olive oil and season to taste. Toss to coat the tomatoes and spread in a single layer; roast until the tomatoes are tender, about 15 minutes. Transfer to a large bowl and set aside.

In a large skillet, heat remaining 1 tablespoon oil over a medium heat. Add garlic, lemon zest, bay leaf, and spiralized zucchini; cook, tossing often, for 3–4 minutes or until just tender.

Remove bay leaf and tip into the bowl with the tomatoes; add olives and pine nuts and toss gently to combine.

Garnish with basil leaves and sprinkle with cheese, if using, before serving.

✔ Gluten-free   ✔ Low carb   ✔ Wheat-free

Nutrition facts per serving (370 g):

calories 301 | total carbs 16g | protein 5g | total fat 26g | cholesterol 0mg | sodium 209mg

PEAS, CARROTS, AND GOLDEN BEET-STUFFED ARTICHOKES

Don't use an aluminum or iron pot for this recipe, as it will cause discoloration of the artichokes.

Serves 4
Prep Time: 15 minutes
Cook Time: 15 minutes

Ingredients:

For the artichokes:
8 large globe artichokes
Juice and zest of 1 lemon
Sea salt

For the stuffing:
3 tablespoons olive oil
2 medium shallots, finely chopped
1 celery rib, finely chopped
1 red bell pepper, seeded and diced small
2 cloves garlic, minced
2 tablespoons sun-dried tomatoes in olive oil, drained and finely chopped
¼ cup white wine
1 cup frozen peas
2 large carrots, spiralized with Blade C and cut into 2-inch strings
2 golden beets, peeled, trimmed, and spiralized with Blade C
¼ cup each fresh dill and flat-leaf parsley, finely chopped
2–3 tablespoons ground almonds (optional)
Sea salt and freshly ground black pepper, to taste
1 cup Swiss, Gruyere, or Emmental cheese, shredded (optional)

Directions:

To prepare the artichokes, remove the tough outer leaves and cut away the stalk. Slice about 1½ inches off the top and trim the tips of the leaves.

Heat oven to 350°F and lightly grease a square baking dish; set aside.

Fill a large pot with water; add lemon juice and 1 tablespoon salt and bring to a boil over a high heat. Lower the heat, add artichokes, and simmer for about 10 minutes; drain well and, using a teaspoon, remove the fuzzy center.

Meanwhile, prepare the sauce. Heat olive oil in a large heavy-bottom skillet over a medium heat. Add shallots, celery rib, and bell pepper and cook for 4–5 minutes, until softened. Stir in garlic and sundried tomatoes, cook for 1–2 minutes, then pour in the wine and continue cooking for 2–3 minutes. Add peas, carrots, and beets, and cook, tossing often, for about 4 minutes, until just tender. Add dill, parsley, and ground almonds; toss, season to taste, and turn off the heat.

Gently push the leaves to enlarge the opening and spoon stuffing in the center and between the large outer leaves; tie each artichoke with a kitchen string and place in the prepared baking dish.

Pour in enough water to cover about a third of the artichokes and bake for 25 minutes, until tender; sprinkle shredded cheese on top and bake for further 6–8 minutes, until the cheese melts.

Serve immediately.

✔ Gluten-free
✔ Wheat-free
✔ Low fat

Nutrition facts per serving (380 g):

calories 357 | total carbs 37g | protein 16g | total fat 19g | cholesterol 25mg | sodium 317mg

MEJADRA WITH CARROT AND PARSNIP RICE

Mejadra, or Mujaddara, is a Middle Eastern dish of lentils and rice, served with caramelized onions.

Serves 4
Prep Time: 15 minutes
Cooking Time: 25–30 minutes

Ingredients:

3 large garlic cloves, unpeeled
1 (1-inch) piece fresh ginger, peeled
1 cup brown or green lentils, picked over and rinsed
1 bay leaf
1 sprig fresh thyme
1 tablespoon apple cider or red wine vinegar
3 tablespoons extra virgin olive oil
2 medium red onions, peeled, trimmed, and sliced with Blade A
2–3 garlic cloves, minced
1 teaspoons of each ground cumin and ground coriander
½ teaspoon of each ground turmeric, ground caraway, allspice, and cinnamon
¼ cup low sodium vegetable broth, more as needed
1 teaspoon raw honey
3 large carrots, peeled, trimmed, spiralized with Blade C, and riced
3 large parsnips, peeled, trimmed, spiralized with Blade C, and riced
Sea salt and freshly ground black pepper
2–3 tablespoons cilantro or fresh flat-leaf parsley, finely chopped, to garnish
Plain Greek yogurt, to serve, optional

Directions:

Thread garlic and ginger onto a wooden toothpick. In a large saucepan, combine lentils, bay leaf, thyme, garlic and ginger, and pour in enough water to cover the lentils by 2–3 inches. Bring to a boil over a high heat, then reduce the heat to medium and cook until the lentils are just tender, about 15 minutes. Discard the garlic, ginger, bay leaf, and thyme sprig; drain lentils, toss with the apple cider vinegar, and set aside.

Heat olive oil in a large, heavy bottom sauté pan over a medium heat and add sliced onion; sauté, stirring occasionally, until the onions are soft and begin to caramelize slightly. Stir in garlic, cook for 20–30 seconds, and stir in the cumin, coriander, turmeric, caraway, allspice, and cinnamon; cook for about 1 minute, until fragrant. Pour in vegetable broth, and stir in honey, then add the riced carrots and parsnips. Cook for 2–3 minutes, then add lentils, season to taste, and continue cooking, tossing gently, until the vegetable rice is tender, about 3–4 minutes.

Serve mejadra sprinkled with chopped cilantro or parsley and a dollop of yogurt, if desired.

✔ Gluten-free
✔ Wheat-free
✔ Low fat

Nutrition facts per serving (370 g):

calories 387 | total carbs 60g
| protein 16g | total fat 11g |
cholesterol 0mg | sodium 53mg

BUTTERNUT SQUASH, MUSHROOM, AND BOK CHOY BAKE WITH CASHEW-SAGE BÉCHAMEL

Serves 4
Prep Time: 15 minutes
Cooking Time: 30–40 minutes

Ingredients:

3 tablespoons extra-virgin olive or coconut
   oil, divided
2 shallots, finely chopped
1 neck butternut squash (5–6 inches long,
   about 1 pound), spiralized with Blade D
1 jalapeño pepper, seeded and finely chopped
2 garlic cloves, minced
3 cups cremini mushrooms, sliced
2 tablespoons lemon juice
1 fresh bay leaf
4 baby bok choy (about 1 pound), trimmed
   and thinly sliced
1 teaspoon lemon zest
Sea salt and freshly ground white pepper, to
   taste
2 tablespoons chives, finely chopped

For the sauce:
2 cups cashew or almond milk
   (more if needed)
1 sprig fresh sage
2 tablespoons extra-virgin olive or coconut
   oil
1 garlic clove, minced
1 heaped tablespoon brown rice flour
⅓ cups raw cashews, soaked for at least 1
   hour or overnight
¼ teaspoon nutmeg
Sea salt and freshly ground white pepper

✔ Gluten-free   ✔ Dairy-free   ✔ Paleo   ✔ Wheat-free   ✔ Vegan

Directions:

Preheat oven to 375°F. Lightly grease a 9-inch square baking dish and set aside.

Heat 1½ tablespoons olive oil in a large heavy-bottom skillet over a medium heat; add shallots and sauté until softened, 2–3 minutes; add butternut squash and cook, tossing often, until just tender, about 5–6 minutes. Season to taste with salt and pepper and transfer to a bowl; set aside.

Heat the remaining oil in the same skillet and add jalapeño and garlic; cook over a medium heat for about 2 minutes, then add mushrooms, lemon juice, and bay leaf and cook until the mushrooms are tender and most of the liquid has evaporated. Remove bay leaf and add bok choy and lemon zest; season to taste and cook until bok choy has wilted, 2–3 minutes. Stir in chives, turn off the heat and set aside.

In a small saucepan, bring to a simmer milk and sage sprig over a medium-low heat; let stand for 5 minutes to infuse and then discard the sage.

For the béchamel sauce, heat olive oil in a saucepan over a medium-low heat; add garlic and brown rice flour and cook, stirring for 1–2 minutes to form a roux. Slowly pour in the sage-infused milk and whisk until the sauce thickens slightly, 2–3 minutes.

Add soaked cashews to a blender or food processor and pour in the béchamel sauce; blend together, adding a little more milk if needed, to get a smooth, not too thick sauce. Season to taste and add the nutmeg.

Add half of the butternut squash pasta to the prepared baking dish and spread it in a uniform layer. Top with half of the mushroom mixture and pour half of the béchamel on top. Repeat the layers, finishing with the béchamel sauce.

Bake for about 15–20 minutes, until golden brown and bubbling. Let rest 5–10 minutes before cutting into squares and serving.

Nutrition facts per serving (410 g):

calories 317 | total carbs 23g | protein 6g | total fat 24g | cholesterol 0mg | sodium 162mg

PARSNIP SPAGHETTI WITH LEMON, MASCARPONE CHEESE, AND WALNUTS

Serves 4
Prep Time: 15 minutes
Cooking Time: 10–12 minutes

Ingredients:

2 tablespoons white truffle oil or extra virgin olive oil

4–5 scallions, trimmed and thinly sliced

2 garlic cloves, minced

4 large parsnips, peeled, trimmed, and spiralized with Blade C

1 teaspoon truffle honey or raw honey

1 teaspoon lemon zest

2 tablespoons lemon juice

½ cup mascarpone cheese

Sea salt and freshly ground black pepper, to taste

½ cup toasted walnut halves, broken into pieces

Hard cheese, grated (optional)

2 scallions, trimmed and thinly sliced, to garnish

Directions:

Heat oil in a large heavy-bottom skillet over a medium heat; add scallions and garlic and sauté for 2 minutes, until softened. Add parsnips, honey, lemon zest and juice, and cook, tossing often until tender, about 5–6 minutes, adding a splash of water to prevent it sticking to the bottom of the skillet. Season to taste and stir in the mascarpone cheese; cook, heat through so that it melts and coats the parsnip spaghetti, and stir in the walnut halves.

Serve immediately, sprinkled with scallions.

✔ Gluten-free   ✔ Wheat-free

Nutrition facts per serving (280 g):

calories 429 | total carbs 42g | protein 7g | total fat 29g | cholesterol 31mg | sodium 38mg

GOLDEN BEETS PASTA WITH ENDIVE AND ROSEMARY-HONEY SAUCE

Serves 4
Prep Time: 15 minutes
Cooking Time: 12–15 minutes

Ingredients:

2 tablespoons grass-fed butter
2 shallots, finely chopped
1 pound golden beets, peeled, trimmed and
　　sliced with Blade C
1 pound Belgian endive, trimmed and sliced
　　1–1½-inch thick
1 pear, cored and sliced with Blade A
2 cups beet greens or Swiss chard, sliced 1
　　½- inch thick
¼ cup walnut halves, toasted
¼ cup vegetable broth or water
Sea salt and freshly ground black pepper, to taste
3 tablespoons flat-leaf parsley, chopped

For the sauce:

½ cup Gorgonzola cheese, crumbled
3 tablespoons raw honey
½ cup ricotta cheese
½ teaspoon red chili flakes
1 teaspoon lemon zest
2 tablespoon capers (optional)
2 tablespoons grass-fed butter
2 garlic clove, minced
2 tablespoons fresh rosemary, finely chopped
¼ cup white wine or vegetable broth
Sea salt and freshly ground white pepper

✔ Gluten-free
✔ Wheat-free

Directions:

Melt the butter in a large heavy-bottom skillet over medium-high heat. Add shallots and sauté for 2 minutes, until translucent. Add spiralized beets and cook, tossing often, for 2–3 minutes. Add endive, pear, beet greens, and walnuts and toss; pour in vegetable broth and cook for 3–4 minutes further, until greens are wilted and beets are just tender. Season to taste and stir in the parsley.

In a food processor, combine Gorgonzola, honey, ricotta, red chili flakes, lemon zest, and capers, if using. Pulse a few times to combine.

Melt butter in a small saucepan over medium heat; add the garlic and chopped rosemary and sauté for 30 seconds to 1 minute, until fragrant. Pour in the white wine, reduce heat to low, and let simmer gently for about 3–4 minutes, until slightly reduced. Set aside to cool for 5 minutes before adding to the cheese and honey mixture and blending until smooth. If necessary, add a little water to get a not-too-thick sauce consistency; set aside.

Add sauce to the vegetables, toss gently to coat, and serve at once.

Nutrition facts per serving (350 g):

calories 381 | total carbs 30g | protein 12g | total fat 26g | cholesterol 58mg | sodium 538mg

WRAPS AND BREADS

VIETNAMESE SUMMER ROLLS WITH SPICY MANGO AND GREEN TEA SAUCE

Serves 4–6 (12 rolls)
Prep Time: 20 minutes
Cooking Time: None

Ingredients:

For the dipping sauce:

2 green tea bags
1 ripe mango, pitted, peeled, and diced
Juice and zest from 1 lime
1 small fresh red chili, seeded and finely chopped
1 garlic clove, minced
1 tablespoon sweet chili sauce
2–3 tablespoons rice vinegar, to taste
1 teaspoon ginger, finely grated
1–2 teaspoons honey, to taste
1 teaspoon fish sauce
1 tablespoon sesame oil
2 teaspoons low-sodium soy sauce or coconut aminos
3–4 tablespoons cilantro, finely chopped (optional)

For the filling:

¼ red cabbage, trimmed and shredded with Blade A
1 carrot, peeled, trimmed, and spiralized with Blade C
1 purple plum radish, trimmed, peeled, and spiralized with Blade C
1 Korean radish, trimmed, peeled, and spiralized with Blade C
1 medium cucumber, trimmed and spiralized with Blade C
1 red bell pepper, seeded and cut into thin strips
1 large mango, pitted, peeled, and cut into thin strips
½ cup Enoki mushrooms, trimmed
2 cups baby spinach
Sea salt and freshly ground black pepper
12 rice paper wrappers

✔ Low calorie ✔ Dairy-free
✔ Low carbs ✔ Low fat

Nutrition facts per serving for the rolls (110 g):

calories 31 | total carbs 7g | protein 1g | total fat 0g | cholesterol 0mg | sodium 26mg

Nutrition facts per serving for the sauce (30 g):

calories 17 | total carbs 4g | protein 0g | total fat 0g | cholesterol 0mg | sodium 30mg

Directions:

Steep green tea bags in ⅓ cup hot water for about 5 minutes; discard the bags and let cool down for 5 minutes.

In a blender, combine green tea with the remaining sauce ingredients except cilantro; blend until smooth, adjust seasoning, and transfer to a bowl. Stir in chopped cilantro, if using, adjust seasoning, and refrigerate until needed.

In a large bowl, lightly toss together the vegetables for the filling and season to taste.

Immerse a rice pepper wrapper for 5–7 seconds in a shallow dish filled with warm water or follow the packet instructions. Remove and place on a work surface; top with ½ cup of the filling, fold two opposite ends towards the center and roll tightly. Place the roll on a platter and cover with plastic wrap to keep it from drying out; repeat the process until all of the ingredients have been used.

Cut rolls in half and serve with the dipping sauce on the side.

SPICY CRAB, TURNIP RICE, AND BEAN BURRITO

Serves 6
Prep Time: 15 minutes
Cooking Time: 18–20 minutes

Ingredients:

2 tablespoons extra-virgin olive oil
1 small red onion, finely chopped
2 garlic cloves, minced
1 small red bell pepper, seeded and diced small
1–2 chipotle peppers in adobo sauce, finely chopped (to taste)
1 teaspoon ground cumin
1 (14-ounce) can low sodium red kidney beans, drained and rinsed
½ pound crabmeat, picked
1 tablespoon tequila (optional)
2 large turnips, peeled, trimmed, spiralized with Blade C, and riced
Sea salt and freshly ground black pepper, to taste

1 small tomato, diced small
1 small Romaine lettuce heart, thinly sliced
6 (10-inch) whole wheat tortillas

For the sauce:

1 ripe avocado, pitted and diced
Juice and zest of 1 lime
1 serrano pepper, seeded and finely chopped
¼ cup raw pumpkin seeds
1 tablespoon extra-virgin olive oil
¼ cup cilantro, finely chopped
To serve: (optional)
Mexican cheese blend (or mix of ½ cup each Monterey Jack and cheddar), shredded
Sour cream

Directions:

Heat olive oil in a large skillet over a medium-high heat; add onion and sauté, stirring occasionally, until translucent, 5–6 minutes. Add garlic, red bell pepper, and chipotle and cook for 3–4 minutes, stir in the cumin, and cook for 1 minute longer. Add kidney beans and ¾ cup water, lower heat and let simmer for about 8–10 minutes, until thickened. Stir in crabmeat, tequila, and turnip rice, and cook, tossing often, for about 4–5 minutes, until the rice is just tender. If mixture becomes too dry, add a splash of water; taste and adjust seasoning and set aside.

In a blender, combine all sauce ingredients blend until smooth, adding water to get a medium-thick sauce consistency.

Heat tortillas according to package instructions and wrap in kitchen towel to keep warm.

To assemble the burritos, place a tortilla on a work surface and mound about 1 cup of the turnip rice, crab, and bean mixture slightly off the center. Drizzle with 1–2 tablespoons of the sauce and top with some diced tomatoes, shredded lettuce, and cheese or sour cream, if using. Fold sides and tightly roll the tortilla; place on a platter, seam side down and repeat the process until all ingredients have been used.

Serve immediately.

✔ Dairy-free ✔ Vegetarian
✔ Low fat

Nutrition facts per serving
(275 g):

calories 412 | total carbs 45g
| protein 21g | total fat 16g
| cholesterol 28mg | sodium
780mg

CHAPATI BOWLS WITH CHICKEN TIKKA AND CARROT-RADISH SALAD

Serves 4
Prep Time: 15 minutes
Cook Time: 12 minutes

Ingredients:

For the chicken:

½ cup plain yogurt
1 teaspoon fresh ginger, minced
¼ teaspoon ground cumin
½ teaspoon chili powder or cayenne pepper (or to taste)
1 tablespoon garam masala
2 large garlic cloves, crushed
1 pound skinless, boneless chicken breast, cut into 1½-inch cubes
Sea salt and freshly ground black pepper
8 skewers, metal or wooden soaked in water

For the salad:

4 pieces whole wheat chapati bread or plain paratha (or other flatbread of choice)
1 small Boston or iceberg lettuce
3 large carrots, peeled, trimmed, spiralized with Blade C, and cut into 1½-inch strings
½ small fennel bulb, trimmed and thinly sliced
1 small bunch red radishes, trimmed and thinly sliced
2–3 scallions, trimmed and thinly sliced
¼ cup roasted cashews, roughly chopped

For the dressing:

2 tablespoons olive oil
Juice and zest of 1 lemon
½ teaspoon each mustard and cumin seeds, lightly toasted
1 teaspoon raw honey
1 small knob (1-inch) fresh turmeric, grated (or ¼ teaspoon ground turmeric)
2 tablespoons fresh mint, finely chopped
Sea salt and freshly ground black pepper

Directions:

In a large bowl, whisk together yogurt, ginger, cumin, chili powder, garam masala, and garlic, and season with salt and pepper; add chicken and mix well to coat. Transfer to a large resealable plastic bag and refrigerate for 1–2 hours or overnight.

Set out 4 (20-ounce) soup/cereal bowls.

Lightly spray a heavy-bottom skillet with kitchen oil spray and heat over a medium-high heat; add a chapati flatbread and heat for 30 seconds to 1 minute per side. Transfer to one of the prepared bowls and push gently to line the bowl. Repeat with the remaining chapatis and let cool to room temperature.

Thread chicken onto the skewers and discard any remaining marinade.

Heat a heavy bottom grill pan over a medium-high heat and add the chicken skewers; cook, turning often, for about 8–10 minutes or until the chicken is nicely browned on all sides (an instant-read thermometer should read 165°F).

In a small bowl, whisk together all dressing ingredients; season to taste and set aside.

Reserve 4 large lettuce leaves and shred the rest. In a large bowl combine carrots, fennel, radishes, scallions, and the shredded lettuce; drizzle with the sauce and toss lightly to coat.

Line the cooled chapati bowls with lettuce leaves and spoon in the salad; top with chicken pieces and transfer to serving plates. Sprinkle with cashews and mint and serve at once.

✔ High protein   ✔ Low fat

Nutrition facts per serving (370 g):

calories 407 | total carbs 36g | protein 33g | total fat 16g | cholesterol 65mg | sodium 236mg

CHICKPEA AND VEGETABLE FRITTERS WITH APPLE TZATZIKI IN PITA BREAD POCKETS

Serves 4
Prep Time: 25 minutes
Cooking Time: 25–30 minutes

Ingredients:

For the tzatziki:

1 Granny Smith apple, peeled, cored, spiralized with Blade C, and cut into 1-inch strings
2 tablespoons lemon juice
2 small cucumbers, trimmed, spiralized with Blade C, and cut into 1-inch strings
1 cup plain Greek yogurt
A drizzle of honey
A pinch of cayenne
1 tablespoon fresh mint, finely chopped
1 tablespoon extra-virgin olive oil
Sea salt and freshly ground black pepper, to taste

For the fritters:

2 tablespoons extra-virgin olive oil
3 garlic cloves, minced
1 jalapeño pepper, seeded and finely chopped
1 teaspoon ground cumin
1 teaspoon ground coriander
1 russet potato, peeled, trimmed, and spiralized with Blade C

1 broccoli stem, trimmed and spiralized with Blade C
1 large carrot, peeled, trimmed, and spiralized with Blade C
1 medium zucchini, trimmed and spiralized with Blade C
1 (15-ounce) can chickpeas, drained and rinsed
2 tablespoons each of fresh dill and flat-leaf parsley, finely chopped
1 tablespoon chia seeds (or ground flax seeds), mixed with 3 tablespoons water
½ cup chickpea flour, divided, as needed
Sea salt and freshly ground black pepper, to taste
3–4 tablespoons olive oil, for frying

To serve:

6 pita breads
1 tablespoon fresh oregano, finely chopped
4 scallions, trimmed and thinly sliced
1 Romaine lettuce heart, trimmed and thinly sliced

180

Directions:

Place spiralized apple, lemon juice, and cucumber in a fine-meshed strainer over a bowl and sprinkle with a little salt; let stand for 10–15 minutes. Gently squeeze out any moisture and transfer to a bowl. Add yogurt, honey, cayenne, and mint and stir with a fork to combine; season to taste with salt and black pepper and refrigerate until needed.

Heat oil in a large heavy-bottom skillet over a medium heat; add garlic and jalapeño and cook for 1 minute, until softened. Stir in cumin and coriander and cook for 30 seconds to 1 minute, until fragrant. Add spiralized potato, broccoli stem, carrot, and zucchini and cook, tossing often, until tender, about 6 minutes. Transfer to a food processor or blender and add chickpeas, dill, parsley, chia seeds, and 2–3 tablespoons chickpea flour; season with salt and pepper and process to a coarse paste. Adjust the consistency by adding more chickpea flour if too wet.

Spread about ¼ cup chickpea flour on a plate; using an ice cream scoop, form mixture into patties and coat lightly in the chickpea flour.

Preheat oven to 375°F.

Heat 2–3 tablespoons olive oil in a large heavy bottom skillet over a medium heat. Fry the patties in batches, flipping once, until golden brown and crisp, about 4 minutes per side. Transfer to a platter and tent with aluminum foil to keep warm.

Lightly brush pita bread with olive oil, sprinkle with oregano, and place directly on the oven rack; let warm for about 8–10 minutes. Alternatively, heat in a grill pan or skillet for about 1 minute per side.

Cut pita breads in half, open the pockets, and slide 2–3 patties in each one; spoon over some tzatziki and top with scallions and shredded lettuce. Serve at once.

✔ Vegetarian   ✔ Low fat

Nutrition facts per serving (250 g):

calories 361 | total carbs 60g | protein 13g | total fat 7g | cholesterol 0mg | sodium 364mg

Nutrition facts per serving for tzatziki (45 g):

calories 30 | total carbs 3g | protein 1g | total fat 1g | cholesterol 1mg | sodium 15mg

BLACKENED TILAPIA TACOS WITH MEXICAN RED CABBAGE SLAW

Serves 8 tacos
Prep Time: 20 minutes
Cook Time: 25 minutes

Ingredients:

For the slaw:
¼ red cabbage head, shredded with Blade A
1 medium red onion, sliced with Blade A
2 jalapeño peppers, seeded and thinly sliced
1 cup cooked corn kernels
1 small red bell pepper, seeded and finely diced
1 ripe avocado, pitted and diced small
¼ cup cilantro, finely chopped
Sea salt and freshly ground black pepper

For the dressing:
2 garlic cloves, minced
2–3 tablespoons lime juice, freshly squeezed
½ cup avocado oil or olive oil mayonnaise
1 teaspoon lime zest
A generous pinch of cayenne or a few dashes
    hot sauce
A generous pinch of cumin

For the tilapia:
4 (4–6-ounce each) tilapia fillets
1 teaspoon paprika
1 teaspoon each dried oregano and thyme
¼ teaspoon cayenne pepper
1 teaspoon ground cumin
1 teaspoon ground coriander
Sea salt and freshly ground black pepper
2 tablespoon extra-virgin olive oil

To serve:
8 (6-inch) soft corn tortillas
Lime wedges

Directions:

Preheat oven to 400°F.

Place all dressing ingredients in a blender and pulse until smooth. In a large bowl, combine all slaw ingredients, season, and toss with the dressing; refrigerate until needed.

Pat-dry tilapia fillets with kitchen paper towels and season with salt and pepper. In a small bowl, mix together the spices and rub over the tilapia.

Heat olive oil in a large oven-safe skillet over medium heat. Add tilapia fillets and sear for 2–3 minutes; turn over and transfer to the oven, Cook for about 10–12 minutes, or until the fish is fork-tender; remove from oven and set aside. Turn down oven temperature to 350°F.

Stack tortillas and wrap them in aluminum foil; place in the oven for 8–10 minutes, until heated through. Alternatively, warm the tortillas, one at a time, for about 1 minute per side in a skillet over medium high heat.

Flake tilapia and divide evenly between the tortillas. Top with coleslaw and serve with lime wedges.

✔ Low calorie ✔ Low fat

Nutrition facts per serving
(185 g):

calories 278 | total carbs 22g
| protein 14g | total fat 16g
| cholesterol 43mg | sodium
127mg

CURRIED CHICKEN SALAD WITH CILANTRO COCONUT RAITA

Serves 4
Prep Time: 15 minutes
Cooking Time: 18–20 minutes

Ingredients:

For the salad:

2 teaspoons curry powder

2 teaspoons paprika

2 tablespoons extra-virgin olive oil

2 (1 pound) boneless skinless chicken breasts

Sea salt and freshly ground white pepper, to taste

1 large carrot, peeled, trimmed, spiralized with Blade C, and cut into 1½-inch strings

1 (about 5-inch) broccoli stem, trimmed, spiralized with Blade C and cut into 1½-inch strings

1 Gala apple, cored, trimmed, spiralized with Blade C, and cut into 1½-inch strings

½ cup each of red and green seedless grapes

1 celery heart, finely diced

For the raita:

⅔ cup unsweetened coconut cream

1 shallot, finely chopped

1 green chili pepper, seeded and finely chopped

¼ cup cilantro, finely chopped

½ teaspoon curry powder

2 garlic cloves, minced

Juice and zest of 1 lime

A pinch of garam masala

Sea salt and freshly ground white pepper, to taste

To serve:

4 large iceberg lettuce leaves

⅓ cup toasted cashews or hazelnuts, roughly chopped

Directions:

Preheat oven to 375°F. Line a baking sheet with silicone mat or foil.

In a small bowl, combine curry powder, paprika, and olive oil. Pat-dry chicken, season, then rub with the oil mixture. Place the chicken on the prepared baking sheet and cook for 18–20 minutes, or until cooked through and the instant-read thermometer reads 165°F. Let cool for about 10 minutes and then slice or cut into 1-inch cubes. Alternatively, use leftover roasted or grilled chicken.

Place all raita ingredients in a bowl and stir with a fork to mix well; season to taste.

In a large bowl, combine chicken with the carrot, broccoli stem, apple, grapes, and celery; drizzle with the raita and toss to coat well.

Spoon the salad into the lettuce cups, top with cashews, and serve.

✔ Gluten-free ✔ Dairy-free ✔ Paleo ✔ Wheat-free ✔ High protein

Nutrition facts per serving (340 g):

calories 445 | total carbs 25g | protein 31g | total fat 27g | cholesterol 65mg | sodium 108mg

CHICKPEA PANCAKES WITH MUSHROOMS, BABY KALE, AND CELERY ROOT

Serves 4-6 (12 pancakes)
Prep Time: 15 minutes
Cooking Time: 20–25 minutes

Ingredients:

For the pancakes:

1 (15-ounces) can chickpeas
2 tablespoons extra-virgin olive oil
1 teaspoon baking powder
½ teaspoon ground cumin
2 tablespoons almond flour
⅛ teaspoon cayenne pepper
3 large eggs, lightly beaten
⅓–½ cup chickpea water or almond milk, as needed
Sea salt and freshly ground black pepper, to taste
Olive oil spray

For the topping:

2 tablespoons extra-virgin olive oil
1 medium leek, white and pale-green parts only, thinly sliced

1 teaspoon cumin seeds, optional
2 garlic cloves, minced
1 celery root, peeled, trimmed, sliced with Blade A and cut into bite-size pieces
2 cups button mushrooms, sliced
2 tablespoons finely minced preserved lemon, or juice and zest of 1 lemon
Flaky sea salt and freshly ground black pepper, to taste
3 packed cups baby kale
¼ cup fresh flat leaf parsley, finely chopped

To garnish:

1 cup baby kale
¼ cup slivered almonds, toasted
¼ cup plain Greek yogurt (optional)

Directions:

Drain the chickpeas over a bowl and reserve the water. Place chickpeas, olive oil, baking powder, cumin, almond flour, cayenne, and eggs in a blender or food processor and whizz until smooth, adding enough chickpea water or almond milk to get a pancake batter consistency.

Spray or brush a griddle or a heavy-bottom skillet with olive oil and heat over a medium heat. Using a ¼-cup measuring cup to scoop batter, cook the pancakes until bubbles rise to the surface, 1–2 minutes; flip over and cook for further 45 seconds to a minute or until golden brown. Transfer pancakes to a plate and tent with aluminum foil to keep warm.

For the topping, heat olive oil in a large skillet and add leek and cumin seeds, if using; cook for 3–4 minutes, until softened, Add garlic cloves, celery root, mushrooms, and preserved lemon or lemon juice and zest; cook, tossing occasionally until the vegetables are tender and liquid has reduced, 7–8 minutes. Season to taste, stir in baby kale and parsley, and cook until wilted; then stir in coconut cream.

To serve, top pancakes with the vegetable mixture and garnish with slivered almonds, fresh baby kale, and a dollop of yogurt, if desired.

✔ Gluten-free   ✔ Dairy-free   ✔ Low calorie   ✔ Wheat-free   ✔ Low fat

Nutrition facts per serving (250 g):

calories 277 | total carbs 24g | protein 11g | total fat 16g | cholesterol 106mg | sodium 128mg

BUTTERNUT SQUASH, CARROT, AND QUINOA NUT LOAF

Serves 8 slices
Prep Time: 15 minutes
Cooking Time: 50 minutes

Ingredients:

2 tablespoons extra-virgin olive oil, plus
    extra for greasing
1 tablespoon unsalted butter
1 medium red onion, peeled and finely chopped
1 red bell pepper, seeded and diced small
1 celery rib, finely chopped
2 cloves garlic, minced
½ teaspoon each of smoked paprika, ground
    cumin, cinnamon, and coriander
1 tablespoon tomato paste, mixed with
    ¼ cup vegetable broth or water
1 (5-inch) butternut squash neck, peeled,
    trimmed, and spiralized with Blade C
2 medium carrots, peeled, trimmed, and
    spiralized with Blade C
1 medium parsnip or a small turnip, peeled,
    trimmed, and spiralized with Blade C
1 cup cooked quinoa
½ cup mixed nuts (such as walnuts, almonds,
    hazelnuts, or cashews), coarsely chopped
2 large eggs, lightly beaten
¼ cup flat leaf parsley, finely chopped
¼ cup almond meal, as needed
Flaky sea salt and freshly ground black pepper
½ cup vegetarian-friendly cheese of your
    choice

Nutrition facts per serving
(165 g):

calories 237 | total carbs 19g
| protein 8g | total fat 15g |
cholesterol 64mg | sodium 57mg

Directions:

Preheat the oven to 350°F. Grease and line the base and sides of a 8x4-inch loaf pan with parchment paper; set aside.

Heat the oil and butter in a large skillet over a medium heat; add onion and cook for 5–6 minutes, until beginning to soften. Stir in red pepper, celery rib, and garlic, and cook for a further 6–7 minutes, then stir in the spices and cook for 30 seconds and add tomato paste. Cook for 2 minutes and add spiralized butternut squash, carrots, and parsnip; cook, tossing often and adding a splash of water if needed, for 5–6 minutes or until the vegetables are just tender. Set aside to cool for 10 minutes and transfer to a large bowl. Stir in the cooked quinoa, mixed nuts, eggs, and parsley, adding some almond meal if the mixture is too moist; mix until thoroughly combined and spoon into the prepared loaf pan. Smooth the surface and cover pan with aluminum foil; bake for 15 minutes, remove foil, scatter grated cheese on top, and bake for about 15 minutes further, until the loaf is firm and the cheese has melted.

Allow the loaf to cool in the pan for about 10–15 minutes before turning onto a platter. Carefully peel and discard the parchment paper; cut into slices and serve.

✔ Gluten-free   ✔ Dairy-free
✔ Vegetarian   ✔ Wheat-free
✔ Low fat

APPLE, CARROT, CRANBERRY, AND PISTACHIO BREAD

Serves 8 slices
Prep Time: 15 minutes
Cooking Time: 45–55 minutes

Ingredients:

1¾ cups almond flour

¼ cup tapioca flour

2 tablespoons coconut flour

1½ teaspoon baking powder

½ teaspoon salt

½ teaspoon ground nutmeg

1 teaspoon each of lemon zest and
    orange zest

1¼ teaspoon baking soda

1 teaspoon ground cinnamon

¼ cup coconut oil, melted

1½ teaspoon vanilla extract

⅓ cup apple sauce

1 egg, lightly beaten (for vegan use 1
    tablespoon chia seeds mixed with 3
    tablespoons water)

¼ cup maple syrup

1 medium honeycrisp or golden delicious
    apple, peeled, cored, and spiralized with
    Blade C

2 medium carrots, peeled, trimmed, and
    spiralized with Blade C

⅓ cup dried cranberries

⅓ cup plus 2 tablespoons shelled pistachios,
    coarsely chopped

✔ Gluten-free
✔ Dairy-free
✔ Paleo
✔ Wheat-free
✔ Vegetarian

Directions:

Preheat oven to 350°F and lightly grease a 9x4½-inch loaf pan; set aside.

Add almond, tapioca, and coconut flours, baking powder, salt, nutmeg, zests, baking soda, and cinnamon to a food processor and pulse a few times to combine.

In a mixing bowl, whisk together coconut oil, vanilla, apple sauce, and maple syrup; add to the dry mixture and pulse until smooth. Add spiralized apples, carrots, cranberries, and ⅓ cup pistachios and blend until well combined; transfer the mixture to the prepared loaf pan.

Scatter 2 tablespoons pistachios on top and bake for about 45–55 minutes, until golden brown or until a toothpick or a cake-tester inserted in the center comes out clean. If the bread is browning too quickly, cover loosely with aluminum foil. Place on a wire rack and let cool for 10–15 minutes; remove carefully from the pan and let cool completely on the wire rack.

The bread will keep in an airtight container for up to 3 days.

Nutrition facts per serving (110 g):

calories 320 | total carbs 29g
| protein 7g | total fat 22g |
cholesterol 0mg | sodium 173mg

FETA CHEESE, SUN-DRIED TOMATOES, AND ZUCCHINI BREAD

Serves 8
Prep Time: 15 minutes
Cook Time: 15 minutes

Ingredients:

*1 medium zucchini, trimmed and spiralized
    with Blade C*

½ teaspoon salt

*1 teaspoon each of fresh oregano and basil
    leaves, finely chopped*

1¼ cup all-purpose flour

1½ teaspoon baking soda

¾ cup whole grain flour

1 teaspoon baking powder

*½ teaspoon salt and a generous pinch black
    pepper*

1 tablespoon honey

½ cup plain Greek yogurt

¼ cup plain kefir (or use ¾ cups yogurt)

2 eggs, lightly beaten

⅓ cup extra virgin olive oil

¼ cup pitted Kalamata olives, chopped

*⅓ cup sun-dried tomatoes in olive oil,
    drained and finely chopped*

⅓ cup feta cheese, crumbled

Directions:

Place zucchini in a fine sieve or colander over a bowl and sprinkle with salt; set aside for 10 minutes to drain the moisture.

Preheat the oven to 350°F and lightly spray a 9x5-inch loaf pan with olive oil cooking spray; set aside.

In a mixing bowl, combine all-purpose flour, baking soda, whole grain flour, baking powder, salt, and black pepper.

Place honey, yogurt, kefir, eggs, and olive oil in a blender or food processor and pulse until smooth; slowly add the dry ingredients and pulse to a smooth batter.

Squeeze moisture from spiralized zucchini and add to the blender; add olives, sun-dried tomatoes, and feta cheese and pulse once or twice until just combined. Don't over mix.

Pour batter into the prepared loaf pan and bake for 35–45 minutes or until golden brown and a cake tester or a wooden toothpick comes out clean; transfer to a wire rack. Cool for 5–10 minutes and turn the bread out onto the wire rack; let cool to room temperature, slice and serve.

✔ Vegetarian ✔ Low fat

Nutrition facts per serving (119 g):

calories 269 | total carbs 29g | protein 7g | total fat 14g | cholesterol 61mg | sodium 172mg

DESSERTS

CARROT HALWA CHEESECAKE

Carrot Halwa is one of the most popular Indian desserts.

Serves 8
Prep Time: 15 minutes
Cook Time: 15 minutes

Ingredients:

For the halwa base:
2 tablespoons ghee or butter
3 large (1 pound) carrots, peeled, trimmed,
  and spiralized with Blade C
1 cup whole milk (more as needed)
½ teaspoon ground cardamom seeds
3 tablespoons honey
¼ teaspoon ground ginger
2 tablespoons sultanas (optional)
¼ cup toasted cashews or macadamia nuts,
  roughly chopped, plus extra to garnish

For the filling:
1 cup heavy cream
2 tablespoons honey or sugar
2 teaspoons powdered gelatine or agar agar
  powder
1 cup cream cheese
1 cup plain Greek yogurt
1 teaspoon orange flower or rose water

For the topping:
1 ripe mango, pitted, peeled, and diced
1 tablespoon honey
⅓ cup water
1 teaspoon arrowroot powder or cornstarch,
  mixed with 2–3 tablespoons water

Directions:

Melt ghee in a large heavy bottom skillet over medium heat; add spiralized carrots, and cook, tossing often, until just softened, about 4–5 minutes. Pour in milk and add cardamom, honey, ginger, and sultanas, if using; cook for further 5–6 minutes or until the carrots are very tender and most of the liquid has evaporated (the mixture should be fairly dry). Transfer to a lightly greased cheesecake pan and press halwa onto the bottom in an even layer; let cool to room temperature.

In a small saucepan, combine cream and honey and heat gently over a medium-low heat. In a medium bowl, add ¼ cup cold water and sprinkle over the gelatine; let stand for 1 minute. Pour in the hot cream and stir until the gelatine is completely dissolved, about 2–3 minutes.

In a blender or food processor, combine cream cheese, yogurt, and orange flower water and blend until smooth; pour in the cream and gelatine mixture and pulse to mix thoroughly.

Scatter chopped cashews over the halwa base and pour over the filling; smooth the top, cover with plastic food wrap, and refrigerate until firm, about 4–6 hours.

For the topping, combine mango, honey, and water in a small saucepan and bring to a simmer over a medium-low heat. Cook until the mango is very soft, about 7–8 minutes, add arrowroot powder, and cook for 1 minute until the mixture thickens. Pass through a fine-meshed sieve or blend with a hand-held immersion blender; let cool.

Drizzle mango sauce over the sliced cheesecake before serving.

✔ Gluten-free
✔ Wheat-free

Nutrition facts per serving (190 g):

calories 343 | total carbs 25g | protein 5g | total fat 26g | cholesterol 82mg | sodium 147mg

YELLOW SQUASH AND DATES BROWNIES

Serves 16 brownies
Prep Time: 15 minutes
Cooking Time: 20–25 minutes

Ingredients:

For the brownies:

⅔ cup pitted Medjool dates, soaked in water
    for 20–25 minutes
2 large eggs, lightly beaten
2 teaspoons vanilla extract
⅔ cup almond flour
1 teaspoon baking soda
½ tablespoon fresh lemon juice
⅓ cup unsweetened cocoa powder
½ teaspoon flaky sea salt or Himalayan salt
1 medium yellow squash, trimmed and
    spiralized with Blade C
⅓ cup dark chocolate, broken into pieces
½ cup butter, softened
2–3 tablespoons mini dark chocolate chips
    or chopped nuts of choice (optional)

✔ Gluten-free ✔ Dairy-free
✔ Paleo ✔ Wheat-free
✔ Low fat

Directions:

Preheat oven to 350°F. Line an 8x8-inch square baking pan with parchment paper, butter lightly and set aside.

Place soaked dates, eggs, and vanilla into a blender or food processor and blend until smooth; add almond flour, baking soda, lemon juice, cocoa powder, salt, and yellow squash, and pulse until the spirals are shredded.

Pour some water in a saucepan and bring to a gentle simmer over a medium-low heat. Place a heatproof bowl that fits on top of the saucepan (without touching the water) and add chocolate and butter; heat, until the chocolate has almost melted; stir and add to the blender. Pulse until mixed in.

Transfer batter to the prepared baking pan, smooth the top, and scatter chocolate chips or nuts, if using. Bake for about 20–25 minutes or until the edges are firm and a cake tester or a wooden toothpick inserted in the center comes out batter-free. Let cool in the pan before cutting into 2-inch squares and serving. Store refrigerated in an airtight container for up to a week.

Nutrition facts per serving (50 g):

calories 147 | total carbs 12g | protein 3g | total fat 11g | cholesterol 42mg | sodium 87mg

GRAPEFRUIT AND MEYER LEMON POSSET WITH ROASTED PEARS

Serves 6
Prep Time: 15 minutes
Cooking Time: 15–20 minutes

Ingredients:

For the posset:

1 cup (8-ounce) mascarpone cheese
1 cup (8-ounces) heavy cream
¼ cup cane sugar
*¼ cup ruby grapefruit juice plus 1 teaspoon
    zest*
*¼ cup Meyer lemon juice plus 2 teaspoons
    zest*

For the roasted pears:

1½ tablespoon butter
*2 medium firm Bosc pears, cored, trimmed,
    and sliced with Blade A*
A dash of ground ginger
2 tablespoons honey
A few fresh mint leaves, to garnish

✔ Gluten-free
✔ Wheat-free   ✔ Low fat

Nutrition facts per serving
(175 g):

calories 418 | total carbs 26g
| protein 4g | total fat 35g |
cholesterol 109mg |
sodium 37mg

Directions:

For the posset, combine mascarpone, heavy cream, sugar, and zests; bring to a simmer over a medium-low heat. Simmer gently, stirring occasionally, for about 2–3 minutes or until sugar is dissolved; take the saucepan off the heat and stir in the grapefruit and lemon juices.Let cool for about 10 minutes, then pass through a fine-meshed sieve and pour the mixture into 6 glasses or cups; cover with plastic food wrap and refrigerate for at least 3 hours, or until set.

Preheat the oven to 400°F.

Spread the butter over the base of a large oven-safe skillet or a baking dish; arrange the pear slices in a single layer, if possible, sprinkle with a little ground ginger and drizzle with the honey.

Bake for about 15–20 minutes, basting occasionally with the juices, until the pears are just tender and begin to caramelize; let cool to room temperature.

Top the chilled posset with caramelized pears and serve garnished with mint leaves.

BUTTERNUT SQUASH AND SAGE CRÈME BRULEE

Serves 6
Prep Time: 15 minutes
Cooking Time: 40 minutes

Ingredients:

½ tablespoon butter
1 (5-inch) neck butternut squash, peeled,
    trimmed, and spiralized with Blade C
3 egg yolks
1 large egg
¼ cup pure cane sugar plus extra for topping

1 teaspoon vanilla extract
1 cup heavy cream
1 (2-inch) piece lemon peel
2–3 fresh sage leaves
A dash of freshly ground white pepper
    (optional)

Directions:

Preheat the oven to 300°F. Lightly butter 6 shallow ramekins and set aside.

Melt butter in a large heavy bottom skillet over a medium heat. Add spiralized butternut squash and a splash of water and cook, tossing often, until very tender, about 8–9 minutes. If necessary, keep adding a little water during the cooking process to prevent the squash from sticking to the bottom of the skillet.

In a medium bowl, whisk egg yolks, whole egg, sugar, and vanilla, until lightened and creamy.

In a small saucepan, combine heavy cream, lemon peel, and sage leaves, and bring to a gentle simmer over a medium-low heat; turn off the heat and discard lemon peel and sage leaves.

Gradually pour cream into the eggs and sugar mixture, whisking continuously. Transfer to a blender, add the cooked butternut squash, and blend until smooth.

Pass mixture through a fine meshed sieve and divide between the prepared ramekins; place them in a shallow baking dish, pour enough water to come up halfway up the sides of the ramekins, and bake for about 30 minutes, or until set. Carefully remove from the oven and leave in the water bath until cooled to room temperature. Transfer ramekins to the fridge and chill for at least two hours.

Sprinkle tops with sugar and caramelize with a kitchen blow torch until golden, let stand for a few minutes, and serve.

✔ Gluten-free
✔ Wheat-free
✔ Low carbs

Nutrition facts per serving (100 g):

calories 232 | total carbs 13g
| protein 4g | total fat 19g |
cholesterol 197mg | sodium 32mg

YAM PUDDING WITH MATCHA-PLANTAIN CUSTARD

Serves 6
Prep Time: 10 minutes
Cooking Time: 40–45 minutes

Ingredients:

For the pudding:

3 tablespoons sultanas, soaked in water or sherry
1 medium yam, peeled, trimmed, and
    spiralized with Blade C
⅓ cup coconut sugar
3 tablespoons coconut oil, melted
⅓ cup coconut milk
2 eggs, lightly beaten
1 teaspoon vanilla extract or seeds of 1
    vanilla bean
1½ tablespoons arrowroot powder, mixed
    with 2–3 tablespoons water
¼ teaspoon flaky sea salt

¼ teaspoon ground cinnamon
A pinch each of ground cardamom and ginger
A few edible flowers, to garnish (optional)

For the custard:

½ tablespoon coconut oil
1 plantain, peeled, trimmed, and spiralized
    with Blade C
2 cups coconut milk
3 large egg yolks
⅓ cup coconut sugar
1 teaspoon vanilla extract or seeds of
    1 vanilla bean
2 teaspoons Matcha green tea powder

Directions:

Preheat oven to 325°F.

Lightly brush 6 rectangular oven-safe molds or ramekins with coconut oil; divide the sultanas between the molds and set aside.

Add yam and 2–3 tablespoons water to a large skillet, cover with a lid and cook, tossing often, until very tender, 7–8 minutes. If necessary, keep adding a little water during the cooking process to prevent the yam from sticking to the bottom. Allow to cool down for 5 minutes.

Place sugar, coconut oil, milk, eggs, vanilla, arrowroot powder slurry, salt, cinnamon, cardamom, and ginger in a blender or food processor and blend until well combined; add cooled yam and whip until smooth.

Pour mixture into the prepared molds. Bake in water bath for about 20 minutes, until golden brown and set; leave in the water to cool, while you prepare the custard.

Heat the coconut oil in a large saucepan over a medium-low heat; add spiralized plantain and cook, stirring often, until very soft, 6–7 minutes. Pour in milk and bring to a gentle boil, then turn off the heat.

Whisk egg yolks, sugar, and vanilla until creamy; add arrowroot and green tea powder and pour in the milk and plantain mixture, whisking continuously. Pass through a fine-meshed sieve and pour back into the saucepan.

Bring custard to a simmer over medium-low heat and let cook, stirring often, until it is thick enough to coat the back of a spoon.

Unmold the puddings onto dessert plates. Serve with the custard and garnish with edible flowers.

✔ Gluten-free   ✔ Dairy-free
✔ Paleo   ✔ Wheat-free
✔ Low fat

Nutrition facts per serving (230 g):

calories 349 | total carbs 49g | protein 5g | total fat 17g | cholesterol 175mg | sodium 63mg

MASCARPONE, CARAMELIZED APPLE, AND MAPLE SYRUP PANNA COTTA

Serves 6
Prep Time: 15 minutes
Cooking Time: 10 minutes

Ingredients:

For the caramelized apples:
1 large apple
1 teaspoon fresh lemon juice
1 tablespoon butter
1–2 tablespoons pure maple syrup or to taste

For the panna cotta:
1 tablespoon powdered gelatine (use agar powder for vegetarian option)
¼ cup cold water
1 (8-ounce) container (1 cup) mascarpone cheese
1 cup heavy cream
1 cinnamon stick
1 teaspoon vanilla extract
4 tablespoons pure maple syrup or to taste

For the raspberry coulis:
1 cup fresh or frozen raspberries
2 tablespoons pure maple syrup or to taste

To garnish:
A few fresh mint leaves, optional

✔ Gluten-free

Nutrition facts per serving (160 g):

calories 376 | total carbs 17g | protein 4g | total fat 34g | cholesterol 106mg | sodium 37mg

Directions:

Core and spiralize the apple with Blade C; sprinkle with lemon juice.

In a small skillet, melt butter over medium-high heat; add spiralized apple and maple syrup and cook, stirring occasionally, for about 4 to 5 minutes, or until it begins to caramelize; transfer to a bowl and set aside.

Pour water into a small bowl, sprinkle gelatine over it and set aside to soften.

Meanwhile, in a medium saucepan combine mascarpone, heavy cream, cinnamon, vanilla, and maple syrup and bring to a gentle simmer over a medium-low heat; add gelatine and whisk until dissolved. Turn off the heat and let the mixture cool for about 5 minutes; discard cinnamon stick.

Divide caramelized apple between 6 ramekins or glasses and pour over the panna cotta mixture; refrigerate until set, about 2 hours.

For the raspberry coulis, combine raspberries and maple syrup in a small saucepan and cook over a medium heat for about 5 minutes, or until the raspberries are very soft. Pass through a fine-meshed strainer and let cool for 5 minutes before spooning over the set panna cotta. Chill until ready to serve.

SPICY CHOCOLATE CAKE WITH BEETS

Serves 6
Prep Time: 15 minutes
Cooking Time: 50–55 minutes

Ingredients:

3 medium beets, peeled, trimmed, and
    spiralized with Blade C
1¼ cup almond meal
⅓ cup arrowroot powder
¼ teaspoon cinnamon
¼ teaspoon cayenne pepper
2 teaspoons baking powder
½ teaspoon flaky sea salt
3 tablespoon unsweetened cocoa, plus extra
    for dusting

⅔ cup dark chocolate, broken into pieces
⅓ cup olive oil or coconut oil
¼ cup raw honey or other sweetener of
    choice
3 large eggs, lightly beaten
1 teaspoon almond extract or the seeds of
    1 vanilla bean
1 teaspoon vanilla extract
Fresh raspberries, to garnish

Directions:

Preheat oven to 350°F. Lightly grease and line a 9-inch round springform cake pan with parchment paper and set aside.

In a large skillet, combine beets with a few tablespoons water and cook, tossing, over a medium heat until tender, 6–7 minutes; set aside to cool.

In a mixing bowl, combine almond meal, arrowroot powder, cinnamon, cayenne pepper, baking powder, salt, and cocoa.

Combine chocolate pieces with the oil and melt in a heatproof bowl, placed over a saucepan with a little simmering water (or place in the microwave for about 1 minute, stirring every 20 seconds); stir in and set aside.

In a food processor, combine beets, honey, eggs, almond and vanilla extracts; process until blended together. Slowly add melted chocolate, pulse until just incorporated, then add dry ingredients and pulse until the mixture is just combined (don't over work).

Transfer cake batter into the prepared cake pan and bake for about 45–50 minutes. Check doneness by inserting a wooden toothpick or a skewer in the middle—it should come out clean.

✔ Gluten-free ✔ Dairy-free
✔ Paleo ✔ Wheat-free

Nutrition facts per serving (145 g):

calories 443 | total carbs 28g
| protein 11g | total fat 36g |
cholesterol 106mg | sodium 88mg

CARAMELIZED PEAR AND ALMOND BUTTER FROZEN YOGURT

Serves 6
Prep Time: 10 minutes
Cooking Time: 8–10 minutes

Ingredients:

For the frozen yogurt:
1⅔ cups plain Greek Yogurt
⅓ cup full fat milk
⅓ cup crunchy almond butter
½ teaspoon almond or vanilla extract
3 tablespoons honey (or to taste)

For the caramelized pears:
1 large Bosc pear, peeled, cored, and
    spiralized with Blade C
1 teaspoon lemon juice
2 tablespoons honey
A generous pinch of Himalayan pink salt

For the topping:
1 passion fruit
1 tablespoon honey

✔ Gluten-free ✔ Dairy-free
✔ Paleo   ✔ Wheat-free
✔ Low fat

Directions:

In a food processor, combine yogurt, milk, almond butter, almond extract, and honey and blend until smooth. Pour into an ice cream maker, add caramelized pear, and churn according to manufacturer's instructions.

Combine spiralized pear, lemon juice, honey, and salt in a small heavy bottom skillet and cook over medium heat, stirring occasionally, until golden and lightly caramelized, 5–6 minutes; let cool to room temperature.

Transfer to an airtight container and freeze until set, about 3 hours. You may skip the ice cream maker and freeze the yogurt directly in an airtight container, but make sure to stir the mixture every 30 minutes, to ensure it doesn't form crystals.

For the topping, gently heat passion fruit pulp with the honey for 1–2 minutes, remove from heat and cool before serving with the frozen yogurt.

Nutrition facts per serving (140 g):

calories 181 | total carbs 20g | protein 6g | total fat 10g | cholesterol 6mg | sodium 53mg

COCONUT APPLE SLICE

Serves 6
Prep Time: 20 minutes
Cook Time: 40–50 minutes

Ingredients:

For the topping:

⅓ cup coconut sugar

1 tablespoon coconut oil

2 large Granny Smith apples, peeled, cored, and sliced with Blade A

¼ cup shredded coconut or coarsely chopped pecans, to garnish

For the base:

⅔ cups tapioca flour

⅓ cup coconut flour

1 cup almond flour

2 tablespoons arrowroot powder

½ teaspoon each of ground cardamom and cinnamon

1½ teaspoon baking powder

¼ teaspoon flaky sea salt

⅓ cup coconut sugar

⅓ cup coconut oil

½ cup almond or coconut milk

1 egg (for vegan substitute with 1 tablespoon ground flax seeds mixed with 3 tablespoons water)

1 teaspoon almond or vanilla extract

Directions:

Preheat oven to 350°F. Grease and line a 9-inch square baking pan with parchment paper.

Add sugar to a large heavy-bottom skillet and heat over a medium heat until it turns golden amber; stir in coconut oil and add sliced apples. Increase the heat to medium-high and cook for about 3–4 minutes until apples are just tender. Set aside to cool while you prepare the base.

Over large mixing bowl, sift together tapioca, coconut, and almond flours, arrowroot powder, cardamom and cinnamon, baking powder, and salt.

Place coconut sugar, oil, milk, egg, and almond extract in a blender or food processor and blend until thoroughly mixed; pour into the dry mixture, stirring, until the batter comes together.

Spread mixture into the prepared baking pan; top with the apples and sprinkle with shredded coconut or pecans. Bake for 30–35 minutes or until golden brown; check doneness by inserting a cake tester or skewer in the center—it should come out clean.

Cool in pan for 10 minutes, then transfer to a wire rack and let cool completely. Cut into squares and serve. The slices will keep in an airtight container in the refrigerator for up to 3 days.

✔ Gluten-free   ✔ Dairy-free
✔ Paleo   ✔ Wheat-free
✔ Low fat

Nutrition facts per serving (163 g):

calories 330 | total carbs 47g | protein 3g | total fat 16g | cholesterol 35mg | sodium 50mg

BUTTERNUT SQUASH ROLL WITH MASCARPONE CREAM

Serves 8
Prep Time: 15 minutes
Cooking Time: 15–20 minutes

Ingredients:

For the roll:

1 (5-inch) neck butternut squash, peeled,
    trimmed, and spiralized with Blade C
3 medium eggs
1½ tablespoon honey
½ cup caster sugar
⅔ cup all-purpose flour
1 teaspoon baking powder
¼ teaspoon ground cinnamon

2 tablespoons cornstarch or arrowroot powder
¼ cup butter, melted
¼ teaspoon sea salt

For the filling:

¼ cup white chocolate, broken into pieces
1 tablespoon butter
1 (8-ounce) container mascarpone cheese
2–3 tablespoons powdered sugar, to taste
1 tablespoon raw cacao powder, for dusting

Directions:

Preheat oven to 400°F. Line a rimmed baking sheet with parchment paper, butter lightly, and set aside.

Add spiralized butternut squash to a steamer and fit over a saucepan with boiling water; steam, covered, until very tender, about 7–8 minutes. Set aside to cool.

In a small bowl, combine chocolate and butter and place over a saucepan with simmering water; melt the chocolate, stirring occasionally and let cool.

Whisk mascarpone with sugar and add melted chocolate and butter mixture, whisking continuously.

In the meantime, place eggs, honey, and sugar in a large bowl, and whisk for about 10 minutes or until lightened in color and fluffy. Add flour, a few tablespoons at a time, whisking continuously, then add baking powder and cinnamon; gently fold in the cooled butternut squash. Spread mixture onto the prepared baking sheet and bake for about 6–8 minutes, until light golden and spongy; don't over bake.

Place a large sheet of parchment paper on a work surface and gently flip the butternut cake onto it; slowly peel away the baking paper and roll the cake tightly with the help of the parchment paper.

Let cool to a room temperature and unroll over a large piece of plastic food wrap.

Carefully spread the mascarpone and chocolate cream on top and roll again; wrap, twisting the ends of the plastic wrap to secure the roll. Refrigerate for about an hour.

To serve, dust with cacao powder and slice.

Nutrition facts per serving (115 g):

calories 356 | total carbs 32g | protein 6g | total fat 24g | cholesterol 134mg | sodium 49mg

PLANTAIN, HONEY, AND OLIVE OIL ICE CREAM

Serves 8
Prep Time: 15 minutes
Cook Time: 10 minutes

Ingredients:

⅓ cup extra-virgin olive oil, divided

2 (5–6 inches each) firm-ripe plantains, peeled and spiralized with Blade C

½ cup honey, to taste, divided

A dash of cinnamon

1 tablespoon dark rum or 1 teaspoon rum extract (optional)

⅓ cup toasted mixed nuts, such as hazelnuts, macadamia and Brazil nuts, roughly chopped

1 ⅓ cups whole milk

1 teaspoon vanilla extract or seeds of 1 vanilla bean

1 ⅓ cup heavy cream

½ teaspoon flaky sea salt (omit if using salted nuts)

✔ Gluten-free   ✔ Wheat-free

Nutrition facts per serving (125 g):

calories 327 | total carbs 28g | protein 3g | total fat 24g | cholesterol 45mg | sodium 29mg

Directions:

Heat 2 tablespoons olive oil in a heavy-bottom skillet over medium-low heat; add spiralized plantains and cook, stirring often, until plantains are very tender and begin to caramelize, about 8–10 minutes. Add a few tablespoon of water during the cooking process to prevent the plantain from sticking to the bottom. Stir in 2 tablespoons honey, cinnamon and rum, if using, and cook for 1–2 minutes further. Transfer plantain to a bowl and let cool to a room temperature.

Place a silicone mat or parchment paper on the work surface. Heat 1 tablespoon honey in a small skillet over a medium-low heat, add chopped nuts and stir for 1–2 minutes, until they begin to caramelize. Transfer to the silicone mat and let cool, before breaking into small pieces.

In a blender, combine chilled plantain, milk, vanilla, cream, salt, and remaining olive oil and honey; blend until thoroughly blended and smooth.

Pass mixture through a sieve and refrigerate in an airtight container until thoroughly chilled, preferably overnight. Pour into an ice cream maker and churn until it thickens; add caramelized nuts and continue churning as per the manufacturer's instructions.

Freeze ice cream for 3–4 hours or until solid before serving.

CONVERSION TABLES

METRIC AND IMPERIAL CONVERSIONS

(These conversions are rounded for convenience)

Ingredient	Cups/Tablespoons/Teaspoons	Ounces	Grams/Milliliters
Butter	1 cup=16 tablespoons= 2 sticks	8 ounces	230 grams
Cream cheese	1 tablespoon	0.5 ounce	14.5 grams
Cheese, shredded	1 cup	4 ounces	110 grams
Cornstarch	1 tablespoon	0.3 ounce	8 grams
Flour, all-purpose	1 cup/1 tablespoon	4.5 ounces/0.3 ounce	125 grams/8 grams
Flour, whole wheat	1 cup	4 ounces	120 grams
Fruit, dried	1 cup	4 ounces	120 grams
Fruits or veggies, chopped	1 cup	5 to 7 ounces	145 to 200 grams
Fruits or veggies, puréed	1 cup	8.5 ounces	245 grams
Honey, maple syrup, or corn syrup	1 tablespoon	.75 ounce	20 grams
Liquids: cream, milk, water, or juice	1 cup	8 fluid ounces	240 milliliters
Oats	1 cup	5.5 ounces	150 grams
Salt	1 teaspoon	0.2 ounce	6 grams
Spices: cinnamon, cloves, ginger, or nutmeg (ground)	1 teaspoon	0.2 ounce	5 milliliters
Sugar, brown, firmly packed	1 cup	7 ounces	200 grams
Sugar, white	1 cup/1 tablespoon	7 ounces/0.5 ounce	200 grams/12.5 grams
Vanilla extract	1 teaspoon	0.2 ounce	4 grams

OVEN TEMPERATURES

Fahrenheit	Celsius	Gas Mark
225°	110°	¼
250°	120°	½
275°	140°	1
300°	150°	2
325°	160°	3
350°	180°	4
375°	190°	5
400°	200°	6
425°	220°	7
450°	230°	8

INDEX